✦

At ten minutes before midnight, a strange fleet probed forward in silence and utter darkness toward the German-held coast. Aged cruisers, reinforced with concrete against the expected avalanche of shells, maneuvered for their final run. Fragile motor launches raced ahead to lay down smokescreens before they were blown out of the water. At sea, huge monitors waited to lob in 15-inch shells, while close to shore a submarine, its bows packed with tons of high explosive, glided stealthily to its shattering death.

Ahead lay Zeebrugge, key to the German U-Boat menace that was costing the Allies 600,000 tons of shipping every month. No matter what the cost, Zeebrugge must be destroyed.

Suddenly a star shell arched up from the dark coast as the German defenses came alive.

On board the *Vindictive,* the assault party honed their bayonets. Within minutes, they would storm across careening gangplanks directly into the enemy fortifications—and in the face of point-blank German fire. . . .

A BALLANTINE ORIGINAL

# ZEEBRUGGE

BY
BARRIE PITT

*With 8 pages of photographs
and 11 maps and diagrams*

BALLANTINE BOOKS • NEW YORK

To the memory of Roger Keyes
and the men he led into battle
on St. George's Day, 1918

'His was the voice of England'

Library of Congress Catalog Card No. 58-13392

Printed in the United States of America

A British version of this book was published by
Cassell & Co., Ltd., London

BALLANTINE BOOKS, INC.
101 Fifth Avenue, New York 3, N. Y.

# Maps and Diagrams

# AUTHOR'S NOTE

I SHOULD like to record my gratitude to the many people who have given so unstintedly of their co-operation during the writing of this book. To the officials of the Record Office, the Historical Section and the Foreign Documents Section of the Admiralty I am particularly indebted, as also to those of the Department of the Chief of Naval Information who dealt so expeditiously with a somewhat hastily-presented manuscript.

From the long list of private members of the public whose memories, letters, and newspaper cuttings have provided so much of the factual and atmospheric detail, I would like especially to thank Mrs. Anne Smee for the material in connection with her father Wing Commander Brock, and Mrs. I. Latham for her memories of her brother Commander Rosoman: Admiral Sir Stuart Bonham Carter and Commander P. Vaux for their help in disentangling the order of events in the canal mouth, and Mr. W. Potter for his confirmatory details and his story of the journeys in in *Iphigenia* and out in *M.L.* 282.

To these and many others I owe the spirit of this book, and to S.D.P. I owe most of the substance, for without her faith, encouragement, and unlimited patience it would never have arrived in final form.

But above all—and not just as a writer—I would like to thank those men who wrote this story in the pages of our Island History.

# 1

THE BELGIAN coastline between the French and Dutch borders is only some 35 miles long. A few minutes before midnight on the night of April 22, 1918, it erupted along its entire length in a battle which, for concentration of power and sudden startling violence of action, exceeded the most bitter and long-drawn agony between the trenches of the Western Front, or even that gigantic clash of the main battle-fleets which had taken place two years previously in the North Sea off Jutland.

Every modern engine of war with the exception of the bombing-plane took part: heavy batteries of the German coastal defenses were replied to by 15-inch naval guns on the British monitors; beneath the screaming umbrella of their fire, howitzers barked, mortars coughed out their howling bombs, machine-guns and pom-poms chattered and thumped, and men fought and died in fierce hand-to-hand conflict with club and bayonet.

The crash of battle was so great and so overwhelming that at one moment five tons of amatol exploded in a sheet of flame two hundred feet high and as wide at its base, without adding appreciably to the clangor: only its lurid, chaotic light was noticed by men fighting grimly two hundred yards away. And out at sea, where its flash was masked, erroneous conclusions were drawn and alternative plans put into operation as a result of the impossibility of distinguishing its thunder from the general pandemonium of the battle.

Seventy miles away, on the English coast, men and women long used to the distant drumming of gunfire, awoke to ponder on the significance of this sudden outburst, and those who rose from their beds and leaned from their windows to gauge the direction from which the sounds were borne, felt hope swelling in their hearts with the realization that a battle was raging miles in advance of the known positions of the Allied lines. Some, who worked in the naval dockyards along the coast and had noticed certain unusual concentrations of men and arms during the past few weeks, or had watched an unusual type of training being carried out by Royal Marines on the chalk downs behind Dover, put two and two together but rarely managed to make four. Did they but know it, a new type of warfare was being born: perhaps it would be truer to say that an old type was being reborn.

In Dover itself, at Fleet House and the Navy Headquarters nearby, those who knew the detailed plans tried vainly to read the story of the action from the distant hubbub, reading failure or success into each climax of gunfire or sudden diminuendo according to mood and temperament: theirs was an inevitable but nonetheless unfruitful vigil, for nothing could be known until the ships came back.

At half past one on the morning of St. George's Day, the clangor reached a climax of unparalleled ferocity which it held for an unending quarter of an hour: then unmistakably, the sounds of battle began to die away. They flared up briefly at about two o'clock and again twenty minutes later, but after that the drumming faded to a mutter and by three o'clock the Belgian Coast was silent.

Later, England was to learn that an operation of incalculable significance in her history had been concluded, but for several more hours no one outside the signalrooms of the Admiralty knew the details.

It was eight o'clock in the morning before any particulars of the action reached the unofficial world. Then, astonished watchers in Dover saw an old, outdated cruiser coming slowly into harbor, her hull blackened by fire and her upper deck a blood-bespattered shambles. She had no masts and her stacks were riddled. Along her port side a tangle of wooden spars and slats hung out at awkward angles, her bridge supported a most unorthodox, shedlike structure which was repeated aft, her fore-top resembled an African native's hunt—and from the sides of all these excrescences hung the tattered remains of

8

flock-filled mattresses through gaps in which could be seen steel plating, scarred and ripped open by shell-splinter and bullet.

The ribaldry which her appearance excited however, was quickly checked. Ambulance cars drew up alongside her as she warped into the dock, and from her sally-ports was carried a seemingly unending stream of wounded men. After the stretchers, hobbled and limped the lightly wounded—and after them, far too many stiff, blanket-wrapped forms were laid out side by side on the quay.

During the rest of the morning and early afternoon, other strange craft crept into the harbor and while the ambulances still shuttled to and fro, some of the crews of these ships together with a motley collection of khaki and blue-clad fighting men came ashore, some still carrying rifles and grenades, all tired, unkempt, their flesh and clothing stained by cordite or shell-blast. They were little inclined to talk, and curiously unwilling to move out of sight of the ships from which they had disembarked. The big cruiser especially, seemed to hold a fascination both for the men who came ashore from her and also those from other ships. Knots of men formed on the quayside below her towering sides, gazing up at her in wonder: when eventually an officer arrived and ordered the men to form up in order to march away to barracks, several were seen to cross to the edge of the quay and lean over to pat the steel hull as though in affectionate farewell.

One of these was accosted by a dockyard worker who recognized him from former days.

"What happened, Jack?" he asked.

The sailor regarded him thoughtfully.

"To tell you the truth, mate, I'm none too sure me-self," was the reply, and then, with a last look up at the stained steel wall beside him, the sailor added, "But it was bloody hot while it lasted!"

By evening, the name of the small Belgian port of Zeebrugge had been added—as yet unofficially—to the list of battle-honors of one of Britain's most famous regiments, and some indication of the way in which it had been earned can be gathered from the fact that never before nor since have so many decorations for valor in action been awarded to British fighting-men engaged in a single operation.

It is as well to see these events in their correct historical perspective. England had now been at war with Germany for three years and nine months, and for all except three of those months the Belgian Coast had been in German hands. From a point eight miles east of Dunkirk to the Swiss frontier near Belfort, the battles of the Western Front had been fought in mud and ice or mud and disease according to the season: Belgian and French villages (not for the first time—nor even the last) had assumed enormous significance in the day-to-day life of Great Britain, and their names had been practically absorbed into the fabric of her history—Ypres, Mons, Bapaume, Festubert, Armentières, and, in 1917, Passchendaele, with its horrific connotation of disaster and wholesale, unavailing slaughter.

Outside Europe as well, the tale on land was of sorrow. The Dardanelles campaign had run its sad story of muddle and mismanagement. At sea, the long watch of the Royal Navy had penned the German High Seas Fleet in the Baltic, from which it had emerged in force only on one occasion, to be beaten back in the Homeric clash of fleets off the ironbound coast of Jutland. The *Lusitania* had been sunk, so had the *Hausatonic* and the *California,* and with the German declaration of unrestricted submarine warfare, America's repugnance had brought her in on the side of the Allies. Pershing and his staff (including a young major named MacArthur) had been in France for nearly a year now and American troops had already tasted action in Lorraine—although their searing ordeals of Château-Thierry and the Argonne still lay ahead.

Nurse Cavell had been shot in Belgium, Mata Hari in France, Sir Roger Casement and Karl Lodi in England, and von Rintelin was already paying the price of his sabotage of merchant shipping by serving his term in the Federal Penitentiary at Atlanta.

Foch commanded the Allied armies on the Western Front. Ludendorff's spring offensive, which was intended to press the Allies back to Paris—and which so nearly succeeded—was gathering weight, and one of his non-commissioned officers, a certain Corporal Schickelgruber, was already experiencing the stresses of trench warfare which, together with his own incipient paranoia, were to bring about mental distortions to plague the world twenty years afterwards.

As far as Britain was concerned, her war-weary populace was conscious only of the fact that somehow they must carry on until Germany was defeated. How this was to be brought about they could not say—indeed they were by now so inured to disappointment and defeat that they hardly expected anything else, their belief in final victory being solely due to a native inability to contemplate surrender. The Government was led by Lloyd George, the armies in the field by Haig and the battle fleet in the North Sea by Sir David Beatty: really there seemed no exception to be taken to any of them, but there was nevertheless a feeling that a new approach was needed to the business of war, and probably some new vitality needed to control and direct it.

When the news was released of the St. George's Day attack on the Belgian Coast, they found that both needs had been supplied. They also heard—many of them for the first time—the name of the man responsible.

Roger John Brownlow Keyes came from a family whose menfolk had fought in the service of the British Crown since the beginning of the 13th Century. An ancestor of his, together with Edward, Prince of Wales, had been knighted on the field of battle on May 22, 1306; another had fought in John of Gaunt's contingents at Castile and Picardy, and one had been yeoman to Catherine of Aragon and sergeant-at-arms to Henry VIII. His grandfather had been Assistant-Surgeon to the Madras Army, and his father, General Sir Charles Patton Keyes, commanded Punjab cavalry and infantry on the Northwest Frontier and in Afghanistan during the most bloody of the Indian wars. He was eventually given command of the Queen's

Own Corps of Guides—the *corps d'élite* of the Indian Army—possibly as some compensation for the fact that although he had been twice recommended for the Victoria Cross, it had been refused on both occasions on the grounds that as an Acting Major he had no right to be in close action with the enemy.

Roger Keyes was General Keyes's second son, and the first Keyes to elect to serve in the Royal Navy, which he entered just before his 13th birthday in 1885. By the age of 17 he was in command of a cutter's crew chasing (and catching) Arab slave-traders off Zanzibar. He was given his first command as a lieutenant in 1898, when he was appointed to the gunboat *Fame* on the China Station. Within two years the gunboat had fully justified its name in a cutting-out expedition with its sister-ship *Whiting,* which resulted in the capture of four Chinese destroyers during the Boxer Rebellion. But it was not until the following year that the world in general and the Royal Navy in particular were to be given a glimpse of what might well be called 'the Keyes touch.'

The Pekin legations of Britain, Russia, America, France and Italy were under siege by the Boxer rebels, and the main railhead at Tientsin, from which any relieving force must of necessity set out, was also invested by them. On the Peiho River which leads to Tientsin stood a succession of forts, all held by the Boxers with the exception of the lowest one, the Taku Fort, which had been reduced some time previously by an International Force led by Royal Naval officers. It had been an open advance across flat ground and casualties had been as heavy as might be expected.

When young Lieutenant Keyes then suggested that he be allowed to take his two gunboats further up-river without support to attack the next fort at Hsi-Cheng, the reception accorded him can well be imagined, and for some days he fumed to himself and his friends in frustration and annoyance. The final goad was applied one evening when two Russian staff officers arrived on the wharf alongside his ship and asked for a drink of water. Keyes invited them aboard and regaled them with iced whisky and soda as he recounted his scheme for the attack on

12

Hsi-Cheng. The two Russians declared that no force of less than 5,000 men could accomplish his purpose—and then only with artillery support—and walked off his ship jeering contemptuously at "the impetuousity of youth."

Three nights later, in the face of direct instructions that he was not to do anything of the sort, Keyes took the *Fame* up-river until she was abreast of the fort, assaulted it at dawn with a force of one other officer and 33 men armed with rifles, cutlasses and pistols (and wearing tennis shoes), gained an entrance by surprise and blew the trunnions off the defense guns before their presence was completely realized. He then—and he later admitted that he had not the slightest conception of the danger of what he was about to do—laid a trail of black powder into the main magazine, connected it to 15 feet of Bickfords Fuse (all he had left), lightheartedly lit the fuse and retired towards cover. He had hardly reached it when a colossal explosion lifted him off his feet and flung him to the ground several yards away. The blast caused the bank of the river to erupt in a geyser of earth and blew out the windows of his Admiral's stateroom on the flagship *Barfleur*, more than 20 miles away.

It is much to the credit of the Admiral—who had explicitly forbidden Keyes to act as he did less than 24 hours before—that when the position of the towering column of black smoke was definitely established, he turned to his secretary and remarked thoughtfully, "That will undoubtedly be Master Roger Keyes. I only hope he is not on top of it."

He then ordered a case of champagne to be placed in the ice locker and sent away his Flag Lieutenant to find Keyes, bearing with him an invitation to dine with the Admiral that evening.

So the Keyes legend was born. When at last the relief of Pekin took place, Keyes was the first man through the sluice-gates and into the British legation, and at the end of the China War in 1900 he received a most unusual promotion straight from Lieutenant to Commander, an equivalent to that of a British military elevation from junior captain to lieutenant-colonel.

In 1914, he was Inspecting Commodore of Submarines,

and the following year, he joined the Mediterranean Fleet as Chief of Staff to Admiral de Robeck who commanded the Naval side of the Gallipoli campaign and the attempts to force the Dardanelles. The arguments as to what would have happened had their respective ranks been reversed will never end, but Mr. Churchill at least held that had his schemes been entrusted to the younger man, the British Fleet would have reached Constantinople and cut Turkey off from the Central Powers, the Russian grain fleets would have been released from the Black Sea and arms for the Tsar's soldiers would have flowed in to stiffen their resistance and end the war in 1916.

Perhaps—who knows?—had Keyes commanded at the Dardanelles, no one outside Russia would ever have heard of the Bolsheviks.

But Keyes did not command, and he returned to England in 1916, still a Commodore, to find that certain proposals he had made months before with regard to fortifications on the Belgian Coast had still not been carried out, although many people were now beginning to agree that his proposals might after all, be worth considering. Not that he himself was to be allowed any say in the matter, for Mr. Churchill was no longer at the Admiralty, and his successors did not look kindly upon outspoken and ardent supporters of the ex-First Lord's policies. Keyes was employed upon routine duties consonant with his rank, and his next promotion—to Rear-Admiral— came to him only as a matter of seniority.

When it did, however—in 1917—he was again a happy man, for it released him from staff duties and gave him command of a division of first class battleships. The bitterness and frustration of the Dardanelles was now behind him; his first son had been born in May, and throughout a glorious Scottish summer he exercised his command in the tricky and confined waters of Scapa Flow with increasing skill and confidence.

It was an idyllic existence—but he could not disguise from himself the unpalatable truth that his country was not winning the war. As a professional officer of the Royal Navy he could not avoid a feeling of guilt that this should be so. However, he had enough experience by now of the ramifications of policy to know that his own hands were tied and that he must await a change in command.

It was thus something of a relief to Keyes when his old friend Sir Rosslyn Wemyss joined the Admiralty Board as Deputy First Sea Lord. True, Sir Rosslyn was not the man to conceive the brilliantly imaginative strategic enterprises which the situation seemed to demand, but he was a man of drive, of great administrative ability and of a steadfast, imperturbable charm. He also possessed one facet of character as precious as it was rare—he was aware of his own shortcomings. Within the week Keyes found himself relieved of command and assigned to the staff of Sir Rosslyn at the Admiralty.

Roger Keyes took up his appointment as Director of Plans at the Admiralty on September 28, 1917. He was then six days short of his 45th birthday; not a tall man, but slim, shy except in matters of duty, with sharp features and supple, long-fingered hands—a visionary who translated his dreams into solid fact.

He and Wemyss formed a partnership which could hardly have been bettered, each complementing the other. Wemyss was the rock—steadfast, impartial yet ever receptive to ideas, as blandly encouraging as a successful businessman. Beside him, Keyes was fire and quick mobility—all nerves alert: here was passion and vitality—a force to cut and thrust at opposition, and needing for the moment only a point of attack.

He quickly found one.

His first task at the Admiralty was to acquaint himself with the true, over-all picture of the Naval war, and in a few days he was pursuing this aim by studying a folder containing intelligence reports of the routes taken by German U-boats to reach the rich killing-grounds of the Atlantic trade-lanes, together with the confidential figures of the results they had attained. At first, Keyes almost refused to believe the evidence in the reports, but when he had assured himself of the authenticity of the figures, he was appalled. In the previous April alone, 621,645 tons of Allied and neutral shipping had been lost—results achieved by 75 U-boats, of which only two had been destroyed.

Keyes held a thorough examination of the situation, and discovered that despite the extensive—and expensive —attempts which had been made to bar the Straits of Dover, U-boats were still, in fact, passing down the English Channel at the rate of at least one per night. Keyes settled down to attack the problem. First there was the immediate task of creating an effective barrier across the the Narrow Seas, then—as a long-term but essentially more important policy—that of rooting out the evil from its operational source, the U-boat bases behind the Belgian Coast.

Keyes circulated his plans to the officials concerned, and then—being Keyes—set about the always unpopular business of making certain that they materialized from paper into reality. This of course, immediately brought him into collision with the senior Admiral at Dover, who had undoubtedly been doing what he considered to be his best for three years, and naturally resented a very junior officer's pointing out that his best was not good enough.

Admiral Bacon, the officer concerned, was in fact an extremely brilliant man whose achievements in naval armament almost entitled him to the title of genius—but like many men of extreme talent he had his blind spots, one of which was an inability to see beyond the immediate problem. He was a technician and an inventor: he does not appear to have shone as an administrator.

Keyes's position at this time must be appreciated. His task as Director of Plans was to point to weaknesses in the Naval situation and plan for their strengthening: he was not, at the moment, concerned with the carrying out of those plans—that was still Admiral Bacon's concern, and during the closing months of 1917 it became obvious that Admiral Bacon had other ideas.

But so had other people.

The new First Lord of the Admiralty came to the conclusion that sweeping changes in personnel were necessary and on Christmas Eve the fundamental change was made. Sir Rosslyn Wemyss moved up from Deputy First Lord to the Supreme Command itself, and he immediately left London for Scapa Flow for a long conference with his chief executive at sea, Sir David Beatty. Upon his return he sent for Keyes.

Keyes found him standing by the window of the First Lord's room, his eyeglass superbly genial in his square face, and managing to look, as usual, like a highly successful stockbroker without in the least contradicting his appearance as the model Royal Naval Flag Officer.

"Well, Roger," said Sir Rosslyn without preamble. "You've talked a lot about what ought to be done in the Dover area. Now you must go and do it!"

It was a moment of Destiny. Keyes himself was only vaguely aware of the fact that after 33 years in the service, his hour had come.

With the work which he had carried out at the Admiralty to assist him, it was not long before Keyes was firmly in command at Dover, and he plunged immediately into the first part of the task which faced him— barring the Straits to enemy submarines. The system in force at the time of his taking command was the result of a combination of all Bacon's undoubted talents, plus the dogged persistence and courage of the crews of the drifters, trawlers, torpedo-boat destroyers and other small craft which formed such a large part of the Dover Patrol.

It was a pity it didn't work—but upon examination it was hardly surprising, for it was apparently based upon the premise that submarines must always, by their very nature, inhabit the depths, and ignored the fact that it was possible for them to proceed upon the surface. Mined nets hung from buoys, some of which were even lit by gas to avoid navigational hazards for Allied surface craft keeping to westwards of them. To make the seas below the limits of these steel fringes unsafe for U-boats, deep minefields were laid, and when no explosions blew steel wreckage or vast oil bubbles to the surface, success was assumed and those responsible for keeping the Channel free congratulated themselves on their ingenuity, and instructed the destroyers and larger craft to remain safe

17

in harbor during the dark hours so as to avoid losses by enemy attacks.

In the meantime, U-boat commanders had been issued with the following instructions:

'It is best and safest to pass through the Straits of Dover on the way to the Atlantic seaways. Pass through at night and on the surface, as far as possible through the area between Hoofden and Cherbourg, without being observed and without stopping. If forced to dive, go down to 40 metres and wait. Avoid being seen in the Channel . . . on the other hand, those craft which in exceptional cases pass around Scotland are to let themselves be seen as freely as possible, in order to mislead the English.'

In this way, the average of 30 U-boats passed over the defenses every month, slipping easily between the high-standing buoys and across the drooping hawsers which supported the nets. For two years they had carefully refrained from large-scale killings in the Channel itself so as not to incite counter-measures which could close their easy route to the wider seas.

Then one of them, *UC* 44, had the misfortune to blow herself up on one of her own mines off Waterford. In October, 1917, she was raised, examined, and a copy of the above instructions forwarded to Naval Intelligence. Admiral Bacon's reaction to the information when it reached him, seems to have been to place it in his safe and turn the key, for when Keyes first met his immediate subordinates—in an atmosphere of some hostility be it said—briefly surveyed the situation and outlined the drastic steps he intended to take as remedy, he was faced with flat repudiation of his statements. Every executive officer present insisted that German submarines had long given up ever attempting to pass through the English Channel.

Confronted with the evidence from *UC* 44, these officers were first dumbfounded, then appalled, then extremely angry. However, they all forgot their hostility to their new Admiral and were soon united under his guidance in a cold determination to put right the errors of the past.

The nets were abandoned as useless and every mine which could be scoured from the dockyards and conjured from the teeming factories was laid in minefields of varying depths, while above them the patrols kept ceaseless watch, illuminated at night by searchlights and the brightest flares that could be devised.

In the first month after Keyes's plan was put into effect five U-boats were destroyed, one by depth charges, the remainder being caught in flare or searchlight and forced to dive into the minefields where they promptly blew up. Many more were seen and chased or forced to dive. It was disappointing of course, that any should get away, but five U-boats killed in a month made a very favorable comparison with two in two years.

Content for the moment with the way things were shaping, Keyes turned his mind to the next part of the problem—rooting out the evil from its chief operational source. This source was Bruges, and a glance at the map will reveal the prime difficulty facing any proposed seaborne attack on the harbor and dock facilities there: Bruges is eight miles from the coast. Furthermore, the German High Command was very conscious of its value and had placed for its protection no less than 26 batteries containing 229 guns ranging from 15-inch to 3.5-inch between Nieuport and Knokke. The difficulties were considerable.

When Keyes first arrived at the Admiralty, he had found the dossier which held the various schemes for the reduction of these difficulties. It contained much interesting reading. The harbor facilities at Bruges were sufficient for it to form a base for at least 35 torpedo craft or destroyers and as many as 30 submarines. When proceeding to sea, these craft could either sail direct to the coast at Zeebrugge through an eight-mile long ship-canal, or if their draught was shallow, could thread their way through a number of minor canals and emerge into the sea at Ostend. Bruges, in fact, lay at the apex of a triangle of which two sides were canals, respectively eight and eleven miles long, and the base was the strip of Belgian coast lying between Ostend and Zeebrugge, a distance of twelve miles.

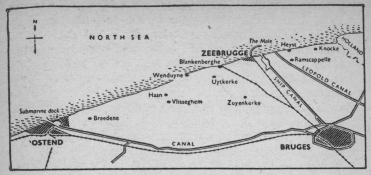

The most vulnerable points of this system were the canal-mouth at Zeebrugge and the basin and lock which lay some half mile inland from it, and upon this area attention had been focused ever since it fell into enemy hands. Even before that, at the outbreak of the war, Keyes as Commodore of Submarines had warned that the harbor installations should not be allowed to fall undamaged into enemy hands. But Army Command had assured him—rather condescendingly—that within three months the Allies would be sweeping the Germans back and would need the canal and its inland harbor for themselves. Now the same authority—though not, in fairness, the same people—looked hopefully to him for the solution of a problem which need never have existed.

Not that Keyes was the first to attempt to solve that problem, for as soon as it was realized that the army was in France on a more permanent basis than had been hoped, the schemes for an attack on Zeebrugge came in fast. Among these were several suggested by the fertile imagination of Admiral Bacon, in whose area of responsibility the problem was posed and who, as a result, was able to put some of his schemes into practice.

From first to last, Bacon was a believer in the use of heavy guns—many of his inventions were concerned with their mounting, transport, elevation, or traversing: though apparently he was not over-concerned with where the projectiles fell, as long as the guns themselves were solidly emplaced and could fire with ease all round the compass. In May, 1917, after nearly three months of careful pre-

paration and three false starts, a long-range bombardment of Zeebrugge took place by the 15-inch guns of a
flotilla of Dover monitors, during which 185 shells were
fired, only 40 of which fell in the neighborhood of their
target. Later it was discovered that, due to errors in the
range-finding equipment, the range fired was nearly four
thousand yards too great.

Undaunted, he was soon suggesting a variation of this
bombardment scheme whereby three monitors, operating
from behind a smoke screen and each carrying one 18-
inch gun on a special mounting designed by him (it
worked: by the end of the war, one such vessel at least
was in commission), should open fire at the lock-gates
from 24,000 yards. It took Keyes to point out that apart
from the enormous odds against hitting a lock-gate at that
range, both pairs of gates were provided with massive
concrete shelters and immediately a bombardment
commenced, one pair of gates anyway would be run back
into protection. As it was part of Bacon's plan that the
bombardment should take place at high tide, there was
in fact no reason why both pairs shouldn't be well under
cover.

Despite this, Bacon remained convinced that the solution lay in long-range destruction of the lock, and offered
his most stupendous project, his 'Great Landing.' In part,
this was a variation of the 18-inch gun bombardment,
but now the artillery was to be shore-based. First a
large-scale landing of troops should take place on the
Belgian coast, then this 70-foot-long, 150-ton mon-
ster, having crossed the Channel on a Monitor, was to be
ferried ashore on a specially-constructed pontoon, taken
over-land to the village of Westende and there installed
*inside* the Palace Hotel.

"The shooting of the 18-inch guns [*sic*] from shore
emplacements," Bacon says in *Dover Patrol, 1915-19,*
"should have been so accurate that the destruction of the
lockgates should have been a matter of comparatively
few rounds."

Unfortunately, although the notes and directions for
the transport across the sea and the installation of the
gun in the hotel are copious and detailed, those con-

21

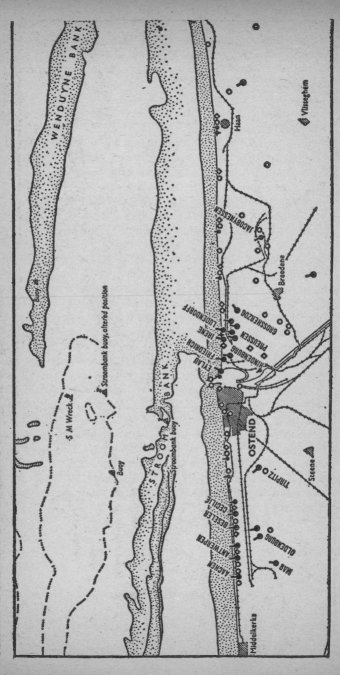

GERMAN DEFENSES ON BELGIAN COAST

WESTERN SECTOR

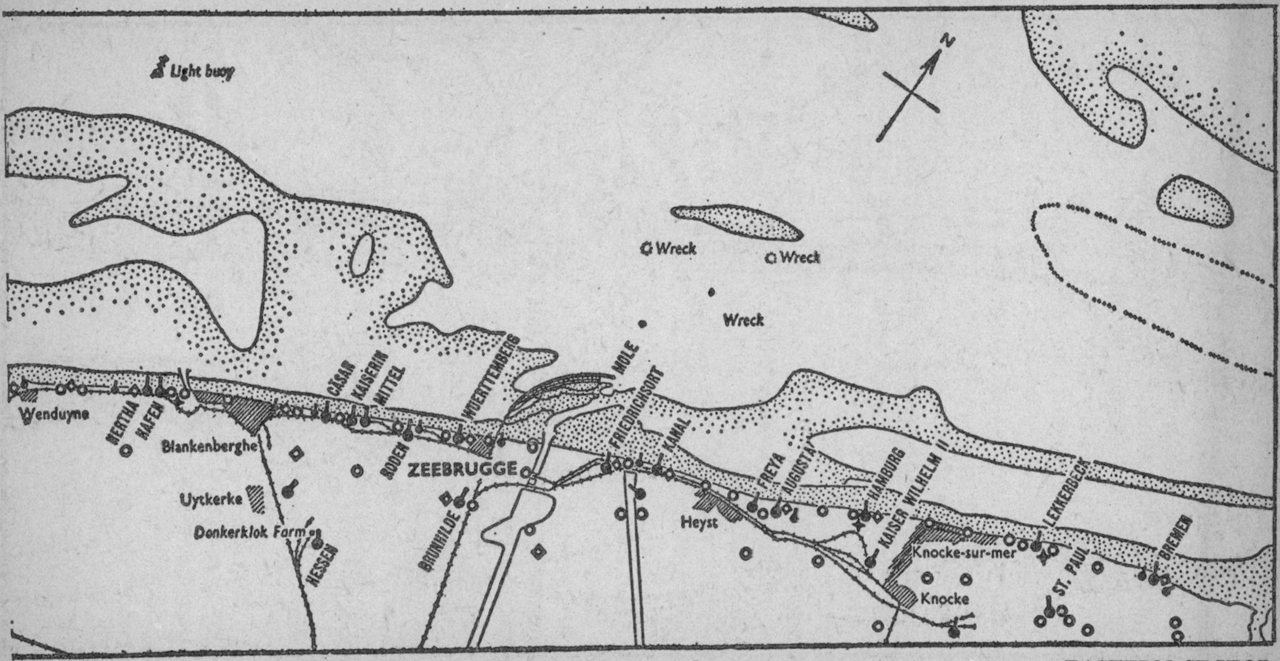
Light buoy
N
Wreck
Wreck
Wreck
Wenduyne
HERTHA
HAFEN
Blankenberghe
Uytkerke
Donkerklok Farm
HESSEN
CÄSAR
KAISERIN
MITTEL
RODEN
ZEEBRUGGE
WUERTTEMBERG
BRUNHILDE
MOLE
FRIEDRICHSORT
KANAL
Heyst
FREYA
AUGUSTA
HAMBURG
KAISER WILHELM II
Knocke-sur-mer
Knocke
LEKKERBECK
ST. PAUL
BREMEN
Heavy guns
Light guns
Machine-guns and Gatling guns
Star-shell guns
Searchlights.
Railways
5 fathom line
Shoals

EASTERN SECTOR

cerned with the actual landing of the troops in the face of the concentrated opposition which was known to exist, seem to possess gaps—some of them so unaccountable as to suggest that a major part of the scheme is missing.

But not all the schemes in the dossier were the inspirations of Admiral Bacon.

Commodore Tyrwhitt had produced one, containing the first suggestions of an attempt to sail a vessel right into the canal-mouth. He suggested the destruction of the locks by a blockship advancing under cover of a bombardment, a smoke screen and a creeping cloud of poison gas. The objections to this lay in the critical dependence of smoke or gas upon the lightest vagaries of the weather, and Commodore Tyrwhitt later incorporated the essentials into another plan for an assault on Zeebrugge Mole from the east—inside the sweep of the Mole—followed by the capture and occupation of Zeebrugge itself. The demolition of the locks would then take place unless it was found that the position could be held permanently, in which unlikely eventuality Zeebrugge should be fortified and used as a raiding base.

Now the first nucleus of a practical scheme was present, although upon this occasion a rebuff was suffered when the plan was submitted to Admiral Bacon for his opinion. His report upon it, dated May 17, 1917, stated shortly that as a military operation the scheme was impracticable, but as a raid—merely to seize the Mole, destroy the locks and then retire—the operation was worth considering.

There the matter had rested until Keyes arrived at the Admiralty and took up his position as Director of Plans. Then followed the interviews with Jellicoe, the Staff Appreciation, and the request that Admiral Bacon put forward yet more plans for offensive action in the Narrow Seas.

One cannot help reflecting when reading through any of Bacon's schemes that if only he had possessed one half of Keyes's perseverance and stern self-discipline, then it would have been his name instead of his successor's which is so immemorially linked with the glories of the Dover Patrol. At times, Bacon showed flashes of sheer

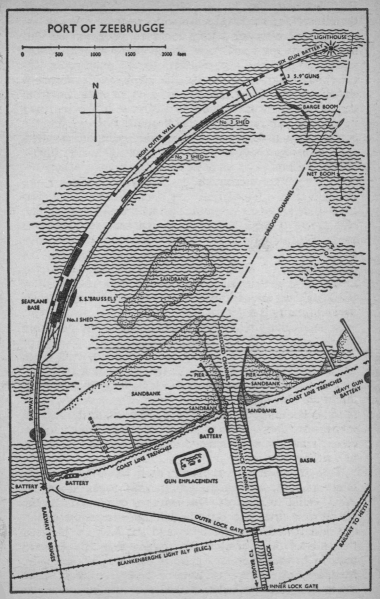

# PORT OF ZEEBRUGGE

0    500    1000    1500    2000 feet

N

LIGHTHOUSE

SIX GUN BATTERY

3 5.9" GUNS

BARGE BOOM

NET BOOM

HIGH OUTER WALL

No 3 SHED

No 2 SHED

DREDGED CHANNEL

SANDBANK

HALO

SEAPLANE BASE

S.S. "BRUSSELS"

No.1 SHED

SANDBANK

DREDGED CHANNEL

PIER

PIER

SANDBANK

RAILWAY VIADUCT

SANDBANK

SANDBANK

SANDBANK

COAST LINE TRENCHES

HEAVY GUN BATTERY

BATTERY

ENTRANCE CHANNEL

COAST LINE TRENCHES

GUN EMPLACEMENTS

BASIN

BATTERY

BATTERY

RAILWAY TO BRUGES

OUTER LOCK GATE

RAILWAY TO HEYST

BLANKENBERGHE LIGHT RLY (ELEC.)

TO BRUGES

THE LOCK

INNER LOCK GATE

27

close and point-blank fire—and with the probable difficulties of maneuver before actually entering the canal, it would be expecting a lot for the ship to be steaming as much as eight knots. In the four minutes required to cover the distance at this speed, and under the fire which could be concentrated upon her, it would be extraordinary if she reached her destination anything but a drifting, rudderless hulk. It was far more likely that she would reach the canal bottom first.

The alternative to ramming the lock-gates was to block the entrance, and in theory this meant that the blockships would have to enter between the piers marking the ends of the *estacades,* steam at least twice their own length between the arms until they reached the coastline, then endeavor to turn and sink themselves broadside across the canal. This came near enough to a naval impossibility to render further examination unprofitable, but in practice the shifting sands which helped the defenders out at sea, might help the attackers inshore.

Aerial photographs revealed that due to inefficient dredging operations carried out under the German occupation, silt had accumulated in the canal mouth until it banked high on each side of a deep central channel. It was possible that blockships could be sunk at an angle across this central channel, with their bows and sterns driven as far as possible into the banks on each side; then further silt would accumulate until the whole width of the canal was full.

Even so, there was still the problem of placing the blockships in exact position. On a fine day, with lots of time, powerful up-to-date engines and a handy vessel, it would be an interesting problem of some complexity. On a pitch-black night, however, in the teeth of alert and concentrated enemy artillery those aboard would face a very different picture: just how different being one of those factors referred to in military textbooks as 'an imponderable of war'.

So much for the canal mouth—now for the gigantic Mole which guards it.

Zeebrugge Mole is still the largest in the world. It leaves the coastline half a mile west of the canal entrance and curves northeast in a mile-and-a-half long arc, of approximately a mile radius. Its total length is nearly one and two-thirds miles. This length is divided into four main sections: first a 300-yard-long causeway juts from the coast and carries a footway, a roadway and a double-track railway extension of the main European system, all continuing directly on to a steel viaduct. This viaduct takes the railway—still double-track—and a raised footpath across a gap which is also 300 yards long, the purpose of the gap being to allow a tidal flow through the Mole to scour the artificial harbor and prevent it silting up into an enormous sand flat.

At the outer end of the viaduct is the main mass of the Mole proper, nearly 250 feet wide and over a mile long. On the outer or seaward side, a concrete wall nearly 16 feet high and ten feet thick protects this area from the wind: along its top runs a nine-foot-wide parapet roadway which is in turn protected from the weather by another parapet four feet high. At high tide, the top of this second parapet is 30 feet—or the height of an average two-story house—above the surface of the water, and it would be some 15 or 16 feet higher than the deck of an assault ship.

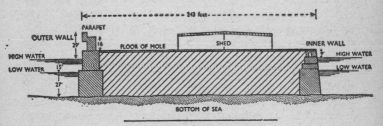

SECTION OF MOLE through No 3 shed

Beyond the end of the Mole the breakwater continues, a narrow stone pier carrying the parapet roadway, now widened to 15 feet and still protected by a four-foot parapet. At its end is a lighthouse. The length is 360 yards, and on it the Germans were believed to have mounted two 3.5-inch guns and four 4.1-inch, all able to fire around the compass except insofar as they masked each other. They were also reputed to have placed a 6-inch

29

Verey cannon adjacent to the lighthouse. The darkness of the blackest night could thus be turned in a moment into the blaze of high noon, and vessels bound for the canal would be under direct artillery fire from the moment they were seen until they sank—by enemy gunfire or self-sabotage.

Aerial photographs indicated other heavy guns (5.9-inch) on the Mole itself—and these were even more menacingly placed, for any vessel rounding the lighthouse would come directly into their sights at point-blank range. Immediately behind these guns, the Germans had constructed stone trenches, antiaircraft and machine-gun pits and well sited blockhouses, all surrounded with barbed-wire entanglements constructed with thoroughness and efficiency.

The peacetime installations on the Mole proper included a railway station, two large warehouses, and unloading facilities for ocean-going vessels which could moor along the whole length of the inner side. To these the Germans had added four large hangars, a seaplane base 200 yards long, an overhanging submarine shelter and concrete-walled living accommodations for the thousand men who composed the permanent garrison.

Keyes looked long and hard at these defenses. He had helped land the Seventh Division and later the Second Cavalry Division on Zeebrugge Mole in the early months of the war, and had carried out a thorough inspection of the place. Now, with the aerial photographs provided by the Royal Naval Air Service and the latest intelligence reports, he was able to visualize the main alterations and thus form an accurate picture of the entire area.

An innate sense of tactics pointed out to him the few weak links in the enemy chain of defense—gradually he found himself concentrating on the concrete-walled living quarters which the Germans had erected inside the fortified area at the far end of the Mole. One such building was within easy striking distance of both the Mole-end guns and the battery strung along the length of the extension; its flat roof appeared to be on—or certainly very little below—the level of the parapet roadway.

Here lay the Achilles' Heel of the defense.

From the first, Keyes seems to have felt that Tyrwhitt's suggestion regarding blockships in the canal mouth would eventually prove to be the correct solution of the problem. What were the main difficulties of putting them there? First—navigational problems and mines; second—the pulverizing weight of fire which could be directed upon an approaching fleet from the heavy shore batteries; third—the artillery and automatic fire of the garrisons on the Mole, together with those grouped about the canal mouth itself.

As regards the first obstacle, he was content for the moment to assume that the navigational experts of the Royal Navy could both find a deep passage to the canal and also pilot any ship that floated along it.

That left the guns.

If they could not be silenced, then their attention must be diverted from the main striking power of the attack—the blockships. The heavy shore batteries could be attacked by 15-inch monitors, possibly 18-inch if Admiral Bacon's proposal could be put into effect in time. Regular bombardments on several nights before the actual operation—always beginning at the same time and continuing for a specific period—might lull the enemy into acceptance of a normal practice, thus slowing their reactions to closer engagement.

Now for the Mole itself.

The Mole-end guns and the extension battery must be silenced before the blockships came into their sights. A well-timed assault of infantry upon the gun positions seemed likely to cause sufficient disruption and chaos to distract even further the attention of shore-based personnel from possible dangers to the canal mouth.

The Germans had erected strong defenses to protect the Mole gun positions from all sides—but not from above. If an assault ship could go alongside the outer wall of the Mole at the junction of the Mole Extension with the Mole proper, and men could surmount the parapet and reach the parapet roadway, some of them could then advance outwards along the extension and destroy the 4.1's and 3.5's, while others crossed the roof of the adjacent living quarters, dropped down on to the Mole

31

end and attacked the 5.9-inch guns covering the light-house approach.

They would then be *inside* the fortified zone. From there they could attack the machine-gun posts from the rear, quite possibly advance out through the barbed wire and on down the Mole, where they could then sabotage enemy and dock installations, thereby creating conditions which would divert the enemy's attentions even further from possible threats to the canal. With perfect conditions and the absolute maximum of success, the block-ships would be almost inside the canal before the enemy realized the intention which lay behind the operation.

With perfect conditions that is; and an absolute maximum of initial success which could only be brought about by super-human efficiency and split-second timing.

Even then, all would depend upon the assault craft reaching its exact destination, intact and still seaworthy, for it, too, would have to face the artillery fire before it could clear the way for the blockships.

Nevertheless, Keyes now had the skeleton of a plan: it remained to be seen whether the practical details would fit closely enough together to form a complete and oper-able body.

# 2

ONE OF the most important decisions, and one which had to be made very early in the preparations, was that of selecting the ship to carry the Mole assault parties. With the idea already formed in his mind on where to attack the Mole, some of the qualities necessary in the boarding craft became evident. At first, attempts were made to secure for the task one of the fast, shallow-draught vessels with high free-board and stout build such as were used on packet-runs, and so bumpkined to go alongside stone quays. None of these were available, and Keyes, unwilling to let time go by, reviewed the vessels under his command or otherwise within his grasp.

As part of the Staff Appreciation carried out the previous month at the Admiralty, it had been decided that some outdated light cruisers would serve admirably for blockships, and further investigations had revealed that eight of those built under the Naval Defence Act of 1889 could be spared. Finally, Admiral Wemyss approved the use of *Vindictive, Thetis, Intrepid, Iphigenia, Brilliant,* and *Sirius.* At the time when Keyes was faced with the choice of an assault craft, *Vindictive* was lying in Chatham Dockyard, awaiting final decision as to her future.

Keyes went to Chatham and examined her. He had been squadron mates with her sister ship *Arrogant* when the latter had been proving her worth as a fleet tender, taking disabled ships in tow, carrying out the rough maid-of-all-work duties which demand sturdiness of build and handiness in all weathers. *Arrogant* was already under Keyes's command—but fully and importantly engaged as parent ship to the Dover motor launches and a flotilla of 'E' class submarines—and could not be spared. In these circumstances, Keyes decided to use *Vindictive* as the assault craft and ordered plans to be drawn up for her adaptation to this purpose.

There is in existence a photograph of *Vindictive,* taken in 1898, the year she was commissioned. Even then she must have looked uncommonly homely and utilitarian, with none of the pomp and majesty of earlier ships-of-the-line. Three funnels rose up rather pompously amidships, among a forest of gigantic ventilators peering around like myopic seals. She had two incongruously slender masts which appeared to have been left over after the construction of the latest tea-clipper, and funnels, masts and ventilators were all mounted in a hull which sat aggressively high in the water.

Obviously there was much to be done to her before she could undertake this new task. At this crucial juncture there arrived on the scene a Lieutenant-Commander R. Rosoman, of whom Keyes had heard much, but whom he had never previously met. This was surprising, for the two officers had much in common. Rosoman was three years younger than Keyes, and like him had trained under sail—in Rosoman's case, a return-trip to Australia in a windjammer when he was sixteen. He had secured his Master's Certificate, then in 1897 he transferred to the Navy in response to a sudden demand for executive officers. He had spent the early years of the century in the China Seas and the early months of the war in the Heliogoland Bight, where he had suffered the misfortune of having the cruiser *Hawke* torpedoed under him; it was due solely to his efforts that there were any survivors at all from this tragedy.

This was the occasion which had first brought Rosoman's organizational ability to Keyes's notice. At their first interview Keyes took an instant liking to him—as did most people, for Rosoman was a man of twinkling humor—cancelled his appointment to the *Arrogant* and sent him off treading on air as First Lieutenant of the *Vindictive*. He had been given full instructions as to what alterations were to be carried out on the ship, and confidential information as to why: here was a task which would test his ingenuity to the full.

But *Vindictive* did possess one grave handicap—her draught was against her, and if on the run in towards the Mole she had to cross a shallow minefield, crucial trouble

34

might follow unless supporting craft for her particular duty were in attendance. Large packets were apparently unavailable—but the same might not be true of smaller ones, and Keyes sent one of his staff, Captain H. C. Grant, upon a tour of the ports. Grant returned eventually with photographs and particulars of two Mersey-side ferryboats, the *Iris* and the *Daffodil*.

One of them had recently been in a collision and an enormous gash had split her hull down to the waterline, but despite the fact that at the time she was carrying about a thousand people on board, she remained completely buoyant. *Iris* and *Daffodil* drew about eleven feet of water, could thus be safely taken over any minefield, and having double hulls were practically unsinkable.

There was an outcry on the Mersey-side when the Admiralty commandeered them, but with tales of urgent necessity in the task of 'bringing across the Atlantic troops of our American Allies', the complaints were soothed. Steel plating was fitted to their sides as protection against machine-gun and shell fire, and the excess partitions which gave comfort and privacy for class-conscious civilian passengers, stripped out to make more room for men and equipment.

With *Vindictive* chosen for the assault, the remaining five light cruisers authorized by Admiral Wemyss were ordered to Chatham to be fitted out as blockships, ostensibly for use in Dunkirk, Calais, and Boulogne in case the German spring offensive should drive through to the Channel coast.

With the ships now available and to hand, crews and men were the next problem. Every man in the Dover Patrol who could be spared from normal patrol duties would be needed in the attack, and hundreds more who could not be supplied from Keyes's command alone. With the approval of Their Lordships, both the Grand Fleet at Scapa and the south Coast Commands were canvassed for volunteers. Sir David Beatty, who thoroughly approved of the whole scheme and would doubtless, if allowed, have taken part in it himself, promised officers and men for all duties—executive and engineering—as

35

well as Marines, both for the assault and to man the guns.

At Portsmouth, where *Iris* and *Daffodil* were fitting out, Sir Stanley Colville offered to complete the manning of both craft, and Sir Doveton Sturdee at the Nore issued orders to his Commodore of Barracks which amounted to nothing less than a blank check for all the men and materials that Keyes should need. In short, Keyes's personal reputation and the concept of the expedition were such that the Navy competed for oppportunities to support him.

This attitude was most noticeable among the officers whom Keyes interviewed with a view to serving on the blockships. As the position in the attack would be so dangerous, Keyes stipulated that only single men would be considered.

"It was very interesting to watch their reactions," he wrote in his *Memoirs,* "when I told them that the enterprise would be hazardous, and finally said that the best chance of escape I could offer them after it, was a German prison until the end of the war. With one exception only, they appeared to be simply delighted and most grateful for the honor I had done them in offering them such a wonderful prospect! Then I gave them an outline of the plan, and said that although I would make every endeavour to save them after they had sunk their ships, I felt that it was a very forlorn hope. They took everything for granted, asked few, if any, questions and went away apparently full of joy and gratitude."

Keyes felt that some of the senior officers who were helping him so much might like to nominate candidates for these posts of honor, and asked for their suggestions. Sir David Beatty put forward the name of Lieutenant Ivan Franks from the Grand Fleet, a young man who had already commanded a submarine and also served on one of the highly successful Q ships. Franks, having passed the interview, begged to bring another ex-submariner, Lieutenant E. W. Billyard-Leake, with him as his second-in-command and they were both appointed to the *Iphigenia.*

By this time the enterprise was gaining momentum and

the detailed administrative work piling up. Keyes had foreseen this and applied for a staff officer to deal with it. He had first asked for Major Godfrey of the Royal Marines who had been with him at Gallipoli, but as this officer was unavailable he cast around in his mind for someone else. He then remembered the navigating officer who had served under him on the *Venus*—a man of incredible industry and absolute reliability, whose mind revelled in the minute details of a complicated operation —Commander A. B. F. Carpenter.

He was available at the Admiralty, bursting for a real job into which he could sink his teeth. He responded to Keyes's approach with alacrity, a relief was found, and within hours Carpenter was on his way to Dover, taking— though he was of course completely unaware of it—the first step towards one of the Navy's most indomitably-earned Victoria Crosses.

To him also, Keyes extended the invitation to nominate a candidate for command of a blockship, and Carpenter suggested Lieutenant S. S. Bonham Carter for the *Intrepid*. This suggestion was adopted, and the third vacancy at Zeebrugge was eventually filled upon the recommendation by Keyes's liaison officer at the Admiralty, Captain Fuller, who put forward the name of Commander Ralph Sneyd, who had been with Fuller in the Cameroons.

The account of Ralph Sneyd's interview with Keyes makes one wish to have been an invisible observer. "He raised so many questions, ifs and buts, that I became impatient and said that if he did not feel enthusiastic about it I had no wish to employ him," says Keyes, "—there were scores who would give anything to be given the chance I was offering him."

Sneyd thereupon made it perfectly clear to the Vice-Admiral opposite him that he hadn't the remotest intention of allowing anyone else to take his place—but he would just like to know what it was all for!—and Keyes, whose own youthful brashness had now mellowed to a faintly rueful sense of humor, finally enlisted him to lead the Zeebrugge blockships in the *Thetis*.

But Sneyd was the exception—both Ivan Franks and Bonham Carter received their commands with the slightly dazed air of men who have won large sweepstakes, and then, besieged by envious shipmates for the two remaining commissioned vacancies on each blockship, returned abruptly to solid earth and dispensed their favors with the cold level-headedness which comes to men choosing their companions for an approach to death.

The ships, the officers to command them, the crews— gradually the striking forces were assembling. There were, however, still some technical problems to be solved.

The greatest danger for the blockships and the assault force as a whole would come during the last moments of the approach to their targets. Somehow, a cloak of invisibility must be provided, and with this in his mind Keyes had spent some time examining the current methods of making smoke; it did not take him long to conclude that if his force was to rely upon such cumbersome and uncertain procedures, they would all be better advised to remain in harbor. In his predicament, he turned for advice to the man who had already solved one problem for him, by inventing the flares which now brilliantly illuminated the Dover minefields—F. A. Brock, a man who, in addition to other claims to fame, possesses the now peculiar distinction that he is variously referred to in official histories as Wing-Commander Brock, R.N. and Lieutenant-Colonel Brock, R.A.F.

Brock had been associated with Commodore Tyrwhitt's scheme for the assault and capture of Zeebrugge, for it was he who had supplied the details of the scope and possible effectiveness of both the smoke screens and the cloud of poison gas. In addition to these so far unaccepted aids to the war effort, Brock had invented an incendiary bullet which had been mainly responsible for the destruction of several Zeppelins, and also the first parachute flares, from which those used by the Pathfinder Force of World War II were developed.

Keyes now took Wing-Commander Brock completely into his confidence, and soon a force of three officers and 87 men from the R.N.A.S. Experimental Base had arrived at Dover, and were working day and night to produce a screen of such impenetrable density that it could mask the raiding fleet until within a few feet of the Mole.

There was far more to Wing-Commander Brock, however, than just a brilliant scientific brain. A keen all-round sportsman and a fine footballer, he liked to see to things for himself. His price for his contribution was the right to take part in it himself.

Keyes was most reluctant to agree to this proposal, for the loss of a man like Brock, at a time when at last science was being allowed to aid the country's war effort, could be disastrous. However, Brock advanced the point that a pyrotechnic party under his command—for he was almost the only person who fully understood all the technicalities—could greatly assist the operation with such new-fangled armaments as phosphorus grenades, fixed and portable flamethrowers, and rockets—not to speak of the smoke apparatus itself.

Then, too, intelligence reports had mentioned a mysterious system of metal tubes mounted somewhere on the Mole, which both they and he considered likely to be the latest German methods of sound-ranging for the shore batteries: he was obviously the best person to examine it and bring back a report. To clinch the matter, Brock pointed out that Keyes, too, was a most important person to the country—and he was going on the raid. But by now he had probably won his point anyway: Keyes was as constitutionally unable to stop other people's advance into danger as he was to keep out of it himself.

Another problem separable from the main theme was that of stopping German reinforcements' being rushed to the help of the Mole garrison. Keyes knew the strength of the main opposition against him, and could organize a force large enough to overcome it, but it was obviously better to deny the enemy fresh troops in the battle area, than to try to strengthen the assaulting forces up to some undiscernible limit. An attack on the German line of communication offered the simplest solution. The weakest point of that line was situated in the viaduct which connected the Mole proper to the causeway jutting out from the beach.

He sought around for someone to devise a means of

destroying the viaduct, and to train the personnel necessary to carry it out. He found the right person already on his Staff.

In February 1915, when the Navy attempted the forcing of the Dardanelles, there took place a highly successful raid upon the Turkish gun-positions on the promontory of Seddel-Bahr. The demolition party from H.M.S. *Irresistible* was commanded by her torpedo-lieutenant, Lieutenant Francis Sandford, and Keyes, with a vivid memory of his own youthful ardor, had noted and applauded the young officer's cheerful aplomb. Later, Sandford volunteered for an attack on the minefields below Chanak, when the civilian minesweeper crews—indignantly fluttering Clause 'X' in their contracts—had refused to go in, and it was he who had led the pair of minesweepers which alone succeeded in sweeping the whole length of the minefield under the vicious fire of the Turkish artillery.

"I saw him on the morning of the 19th March," stated Keyes, "almost in rags, with clothes and skin discolored by the fumes of a high explosive shell, and was immensely impressed by his gallant, light hearted bearing."

Sandford was soon a member of Keyes's staff, and only too soon afterwards a casualty as a result of it, losing an eye in an attempt to mine the approaches to Smyrna just before the August offensive. He came home, spent months in hospital, and faced a future of dim, unrewarding administrative drudgery. Keyes, however, exhibiting again the loyalty and kindness which never forgot past deeds or favors, sought him out and had him appointed to his staff with the rank of Lieutenant-Commander. To him, Keyes now entrusted the crucial task of the destruction of the viaduct.

At first, experiments were carried out with rafts loaded with high explosive and fitted with time fuses, the idea being to loose them westwards of the viaduct and allow the current to sweep them in among the supporting stanchions and girders—but it would have been, at best, an uncertain method. For one thing, the rafts would have to be towed very close to their target to be certain of arriving directly under the viaduct—and it was unlikely that they would do so unnoticed. Small arms fire from the Mole and heavier metal from the shore guns would harass the tugs and make accurate navigation difficult if not impossible—and one bullet into the rafts' cargoes might blow the entire unit out of the water long before it was in a position to do the slightest damage.

Sandford solved the problem.

There were at Portsmouth several old 'C' class submarines, fit only for local defense. Sandford's idea was that two of these should be obtained, their bows packed with high explosive, and they should then be rammed under the viaduct—one would be enough, but it was better to have two in case one broke down. Official sanction was given and Sandford set to work. He collected the submarines and 'finding a young married officer in command of C 3, he managed to effect an exchange'—and one imagines, to solve another, personal problem—for the command was given to his younger brother.

According to the dictionary, the meaning of the word 'Nepotism' is ". . . undue favor from holder of patronage to secure positions of profit and gain for relatives. . . ." Whether the term applies to a holder of patronage securing for his brother a position of utmost danger and practically certain death is not clear, but what does seem quite incredibly clear is that whereas the task of transforming the submarines into vast human torpedoes was tackled with enthusiasm and zest, that of arranging for the safe removal of those on board before the explosion was treated with an air of casual unconcern.

When Keyes inquired what steps had been taken in this direction, he was airily informed that gyroscopic control had been fitted to allow the submarines' Commanders, "if they cared to" to take to the diminutive boat which each carried and allow the craft to travel the last hundred yards or so unmanned. "But," recorded Keyes, in view of what happened later, "I do not believe that he or his brother ever intended to make use of it, and they only installed it to save me from a subsequent charge of having condemned six men to practically certain death."

But if death was in their minds, the two brothers were

41

determined to enjoy what life was left to them. As part of the escape plans, they commandeered a fast motorboat being built on the Thames for the French Government at a cost of $90,000. Later, having tried it out—and one can imagine with what delight—they returned it, no doubt feeling that it was too good to waste.

However, a new picket-boat just finished in Chatham dockyard was proceeding to Portsmouth under her own steam, and Sandford seized her as she passed Dover, telegraphed the two respective Commanders-in-Chief to the effect that Vice-Admiral Keyes required the loan of the craft for about a fortnight, and selected a crew of stalwarts with whose help he proposed to follow the submarines (he could not take the place of C 1's skipper himself, as that young man, Lieutenant A. C. Newbold, was unmarried and had no intention of relinquishing his command) and pick up the crews after they had blown up the viaduct.

"I can think of no one I have ever met who carried enterprising initiative further than that most gallant and gifted officer," wrote Keyes, but there is a faintly caustic note about the end of the eulogy: ". . . and it was a long time before my office was free of correspondence connected with his activities."

But now an incident occurred which abruptly recalled Keyes's attention to Dover. During the time when all these preparations were taking place, the day-to-day activities of the Dover Patrol were still the most important duties of his command, and having reorganized the minefield system and deployed a continual screen of vessels across the danger area until the Straits were effectively barred, Keyes had worked out a system to deal with the inevitable German reaction.

This, it was fairly easy to guess, would take the form of a night attack by destroyers upon the drifter fleet—and unfortunately it took place on February 14-15, the only night since Keyes's new system had been inaugurated that there was no heavy monitor at sea to protect the smaller craft. The 12-inch monitor which should have been on duty had developed defects only that after-

CROSS SECTION OF VIADUCT LOOKING TOWARDS THE MOLE

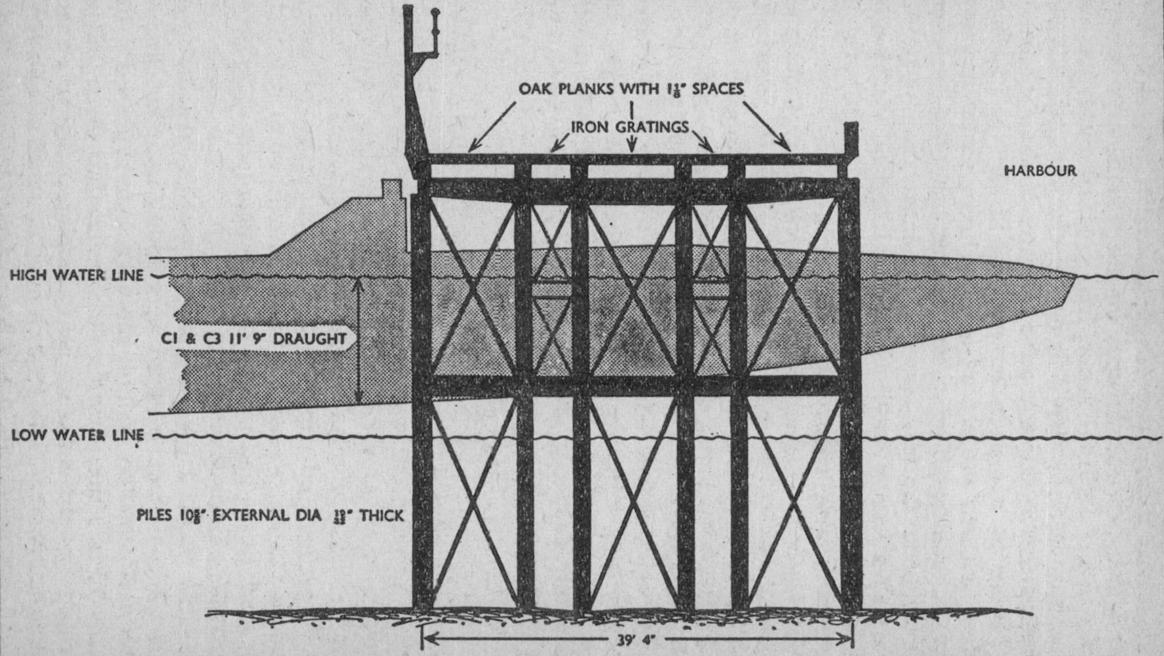

HARBOUR

OAK PLANKS WITH 1⅛" SPACES

IRON GRATINGS

HIGH WATER LINE

C1 & C3 11' 9" DRAUGHT

LOW WATER LINE

PILES 10⅝" EXTERNAL DIA 1⅜" THICK

39' 4"

noon, and all others were either refitting or on duty at Dunkirk.

The events which took place between the hours of 12:55 A.M. and 3:18 A.M. that night, remained for long a bitter memory in the minds of everyone concerned— on our side, that is; for the Germans it was an unqualified success. From subsequent reports and the long process of sifting the wheat from the chaff of German claims, it would appear that two half-sections of a destroyer flotilla, led most ably by a certain Kapitän-zur-See Heinecke, came down from the Heligoland Bight, separated at the Sandettie Bank, and struck one at each end of the line of small craft strung across the Channel.

Like wolves among a flock of sheep, they ravaged their way along the line, met in the center, turned and streaked for home—having sunk a trawler and seven drifters, severely damaged the paddle-steamer *Newbury* and three more drifters, and left a casualty-list of seventy-six officers and men killed, and thirteen wounded. There was undoubted mismanagement somewhere, for Keyes had spent the night waiting for signals which would set his carefully-prepared defense plans into operation, and which never came. In the morning, consumed with cold fury after having read the reports and listened to the tales of the survivors, Keyes ordered a Court of Inquiry and upon the strength of its findings informed the Admiralty that he intended to try by courts-martial the commanding officers of two P-boats, *Amazon* and *Termagant*. Although he had been advised that there was not sufficient evidence to try the commanding officer of the small monitor M 26, nevertheless Keyes wanted him relieved of his command at once.

The court-martial of the commanding officer of *Amazon* was duly carried through, the court finding the charges proved and severely reprimanding the culprit; at which Keyes, his blood up, exploded to the Admiralty at the incredible leniency of the sentence, and the Admiralty agreeing with him, the young officer was in turn relieved of his command and given clearly to understand that his career was finished.

Anyone who knew Keyes could guess what would

44

happen next. The mists of anger dispersed, what damage could be righted was put in order; February passed, and March, with its prospects of hope and action, arrived. Still the fate of the young officer weighed on his mind.

"I attributed his failure to lack of experience rather than want of courage, and I felt so sorry that so young an officer should have his future in the Navy damned at the outset of his career, that I sent for him and offered him an appointment in the *Vindictive,* which he gladly accepted."

The young man joined an eager and industrious team. At Chatham, Lieutenant-Commander Rosoman had been joined by Engineer Lieutenant-Commander W. A. Bury and Commander Seymour Osborne, a gunnery expert who had been one of the first officers appointed to Keyes's staff at Dover. While Osborne re-planned *Vindictive*'s armament, the others worked in collaboration with the dockyard staff and endeavored to solve the problems of speeding the assaulting forces up and over the Zeebrugge parapet and on to the Mole.

It was not just a question of getting a few men over this concrete hurdle; there were to be three companies of Royal Marines (in all 580 men) altogether with a Bluejacket assault party of 200—all far more heavily and cumbersomely burdened than the Commandos of World War II with their automatic weapons and plastic explosive. For the intended demolitions alone—guncotton being the chief destructive agent—a number of wicker baskets on wheels had been obtained from the post office to provide transport.

Rosoman and Bury looked long and earnestly at Admiral Bacon's twelve-foot-wide ramp, which if it could have been carried and placed in position, would have allowed a veritable flood of men to charge down on to the enemy defenses. The idea was right—'Get there fastest with the mostest!'—but it was just not feasible.

However, if it was not possible to use one ramp carrying eight men, then eight ramps or more could carry one man each—but first get the solid mass of men as close up under the parapet top as possible, before splitting them into single files. In order to do this, a false deck was built on the skid beams along *Vindictive*'s port side from forecastle to quarterdeck, and three wide ramps led up to it from the starboard side of the upper deck.

In addition to performing its original task, this false deck would also give protection to the waiting troops, who could now be accommodated under it, on the original upper deck. Eighteen 27-inch-wide ramps were then hinged to the false deck and triced up, ready to be dropped on to the parapet top. High water would be the best time to deliver the attack, this parapet top would be at the most seven, and at least four, feet above the level of the false deck, but owing to the toe of the Mole (see diagram p. 29) and the heavy fenders slung alongside to protect *Vindictive*'s hull from scraping on the concrete, the possible distance to be spanned could be as much as thirty feet.

This is quite far enough, on a dark night, to carry heavy equipment across a narrow, swaying bridge without handrails.

Another problem which faced Rosoman and his co-workers was that of grappling *Vindictive* to the Mole and holding her in position against both the fierce tideway and the surge which the ship would carry with her. Derricks were erected fore and aft, from which were suspended grappling irons to hook over the parapet. In addition, it was decided that the Mersey ferry *Daffodil* should sail under the orders of the *Vindictive*'s commanding officer and would, if necessary, butt the bigger ship into position and hold her there until she was securely berthed.

Meanwhile Commander Osborne had been busy. To augment *Vindictive*'s normal armament, an 11-inch howitzer was set up on her quarterdeck, a 7.5-inch on her forecastle and another on the false deck. These guns would deal with the Mole batteries and, when these had been put out of action, with any other worth-while target which presented itself within range and bearing. The main emphasis in supplementary armament, however, was on weapons for close-range infantry fighting. Three pom-poms and six Lewis guns were mounted in the fore-top to

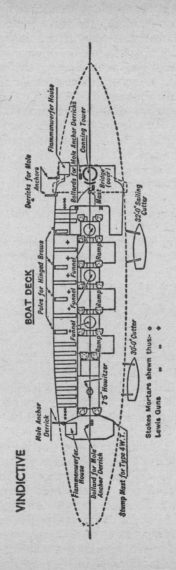

VINDICTIVE

BOAT DECK

Mole Anchor Derrick

Flammenwerfer House

Bollard for Mole Anchor Derrick

Stump Mast for Type 4 W.T.

7.5" Howitzer

30-0 Cutter

Poles for Hinged Brows

Funnel

Funnel

Funnel

Funnel

Ramp

Ramp

Ramp

Derricks for Mole Anchors

Flammenwerfer House

Bollards for Mole Anchor Derricks

Conning Tower

Mast Bridge (over)

32-0 Sailing Cutter

Stokes Mortars shewn thus:- o

" " Lewis Guns " " ✦

fire over the parapet and cover the assault, ten more
Lewis guns were mounted on the false deck between
the ramps, and batteries of Stokes Mortars were set up
fore and aft, to lob their shells over the top onto gun positions or enemy ships moored inside the Mole.

In two special mattress-protected shelters, one abreast
the forebridge, the other at the after end of the upper
deck, the pyrotechnic party installed Wing-Commander
Brock's dreadful *Flammenwerfers*. The conning-tower,
located under the bridge, was similarly swathed and but-
tressed with sandbags. Mainmast and foremast above the
top were removed, and the mainmast was laid horizontally across the quarterdeck, the heel bedded in concrete
and the end extended several feet beyond the ship's side,
to act as a bumpkin and protect the port propeller.

All these alterations made surprisingly little difference
to *Vindictive*'s appearance, which was so sturdily utilitarian that no additional structure, however crude and
homely, would alter the balance or appear incongruous.
She still sat high out of the water, with an air of righteous
implacability.

There was not a great deal to do to *Iris* and *Daffodil*
other than provide them both with steel plating and mattresses as protection against bullets and shrapnel, to in-
stall their grappling irons and also the necessary smoke
apparatus to cover their retreat at the end of the action.
They both carried scaling ladders long enough to reach
the parapet top, but in case of difficulties, the men aboard
these two smaller craft could reach the Mole via the
*Vindictive* and her ramps. Both commanding officers had
been chosen with particular care, for either of them might
well have to assume sole command of the most crucial
part of the enterprise if things went badly on *Vindictive*.

Commander Valentine Gibbs was appointed to command *Iris*—and if there is a faintly musical-comedy atmosphere about his name there was none in his character.
Keyes had met him when Gibbs was a young midshipman
in the China Seas, and knew him for a cool, resourceful
officer—he had won the Cresta Run in the year before
the war.

For *Daffodil*, which was to sail under orders of *Vin-*

*dictive*'s Captain, Keyes chose Lieutenant Harold Campbell, who had served with him during the action of Heligoland Bight.

Plans, therefore, were maturing nicely for the Zeebrugge part of the expedition. There was, however, another exit from the inland harbor at Bruges and this had to be stopped as well.

# 3

"THE NAME Zeebrugge" Keyes wrote later, "has become so intimately connected with the operation that it does not appear to be generally appreciated (even by the official naval historian) that our efforts were directed against Bruges. Zeebrugge itself could never have been blocked . . . My object was to cut Zeebrugge off from the docks, submarine shelters and repair shops several miles inland, on which the enemy were dependent for the maintenance of their flotillas. . . .

"When the operations were undertaken, it was believed that although the blocking of the Zeebrugge entrance was the most important of all objects, it would be necessary also to block the entrance to Ostend harbor, in order to seal up the Bruges ship-canal and docks, for unless this was done the lighter craft would still be able to pass to and fro—more or less freely—through the smaller canals."

There was no Mole at Ostend, but the coastal batteries were just as heavy and as thickly grouped as those around the canal entrance at Zeebrugge. The Friedrich, Irene, and Ludendorff batteries—all of 11-inch guns—as well as the Jacobynessen 15-inch battery, were all mounted within 5,000 yards east of the canal, and the two-mile-long Ostend *plage* to westward was encrusted with machine gun and searchlight positions.

The essence therefore, of any successful attack and blocking operation must be sufficient speed on the part of the blockships to reach their destinations before the German guns could register on them, coupled with high navigational accuracy, for there would be neither time nor room for maneuver. Obviously, Wing-Commander Brock's smoke screens would have an important part to play here—as at Zeebrugge. But it was equally important that once the German gunners did open fire on the blockships, there must be adequate heavy artillery available to reply to them.

The history of ship-to-shore gunnery up to the turn of 1918 reveals a surprisingly large margin of inaccuracy in the practice; surprising, that is, to present-day readers, taking the developments of radar for granted. But in 1918, systems of non-visual ranging were still in a stage of groping infancy (in some ways the Germans were ahead of us) and that other basic aid to accuracy, gyroscopic direction-control, although invented, was not yet in use.

The standard in the Navy as a whole, however, was not so bad as the results obtained during the previous bombardments of Zeebrugge and Ostend would suggest. At Gallipoli, for instance, the Naval squadrons called upon to support the hard-pressed troops quickly re-learned the arts of coastal bombardment and under guidance soon gained a high degree of proficiency.

One of the experts who had contributed to this sudden improvement was Commander H. P. Douglas of the Hydrographical Department of the Admiralty. Together with his chief aide, Lieutenant-Commander Haselfoot, Douglas perfected and taught an effective method of fixing the relative positions of ship to target, and once this was put into practice, at least one of the basic problems was solved.

Faced now with the need for accurate bombardment of the German gun-positions on the Belgian coast, Keyes requested the loan of both these officers, and as they also had returned to England, they were sent down to Dover early in the year.

Their first report on the situation was not encouraging. Although there were small-scale navigational charts of the area, there were no charts of sufficient detail for bombardment purposes. Also, in view of the error of four thousand yards in range estimation of the bombardment in May 1917, there was official disfavor of any further attempts which might incur more suffering on the part of Belgian civilians than among enemy gun-crews.

At a word from Keyes the two men set to work. First, with the assistance of French and Belgian authorities and confrères in the Admiralty, they drew up new, large-scale charts. Then, under protection of vessels patrolling the Belgian coast—generally a 12-inch monitor, a small monitor, and at least a pair of destroyers—they scurried back and forth in a motor launch, plotting the positions of the German emplacements. As can be imagined, this entailed much dangerous work creeping close along the coastline at night, ever-ready to turn tail and flee—for to be caught with their charts and instruments would spell disaster to the entire project. However, they were not caught. Captain Douglas (he had been promoted) then drew up a combination table and diagram by which range and bearing could be worked out almost instantly from given data.

One day Keyes, in conversation with the captain of a 12-inch monitor at Dunkirk, heard of the officer's invention of a gyroscopic director which would make it possible for guns to be laid on any true bearing without the necessity of aiming marks, thus enabling them to fire at night, under way and out of sight of land. Commander Altham, the inventor of this ingenious director, had in fact previously shown it to Admiral Bacon, who congratulated him upon it but took no further action.

Inside two months, Keyes had it developed, taught, and put into operation.

The chance to test these new methods of bombardment came sooner than was anticipated. On March 21, the whole weight of the German Army, reinforced by vast numbers of troops released from the East by the defection of Russia from the Grand Alliance, was thrown against our battle line on the Somme. It was to be the last desperate gamble of the Central Powers, and the Kaiser and his generals were determined to spare no effort to insure its success.

That night, a force of nine German destroyers and six large torpedo boats left port to carry out a bombardment on the rolling stock depots just behind the left flank of the Allied line. They were divided into three groups and instructed to attack the railway traffic east and south of Dunkirk, a section of the track at Bray-Dunes and the railheads at Adinkerke and La Panne; the bombardment to last an hour, during which time they were to pour 1,100 shells of various calibre into the targets.

In the event, the longest any of the attacking forces remained in position was ten minutes, and less than a sixth of their ammunition was even loaded into the guns.

At the moment when the Germans opened fire, Allied Naval shipping in Dunkirk (which came under Keyes's command irrespective of whether the units were British or French) were all outside Dunkirk harbor, having cleared out during an air raid. In any case, the duty vessels were at their posts—the 15-inch Monitor *Terror*, the small monitor *M 26* and the French destroyer *Oriflamme* were in the Potje off La Panne itself, and the destroyers *Morris* (British), *Capitaine Mehl, Magon,* and *Bouclier* were standing by in the Durkirk Roads, newly-joined by the flotilla leader *Botha*—with the two hydrographical officers still actually on board, after one of their surreptitious inspections of the Belgian coast.

At 3:50 A.M. the enemy opened fire. Before they had time to let go with their second salvo, *Botha* had slipped her cables and was steaming northeast to cut them off from their base, while *Terror* was firing star-shell, followed immediately by a salvo from her 6-inch guns. The nearest of the enemy destroyers saw the Allied flotillas in the *Terror*'s star-shell (the French destroyers were off the mark only a matter of seconds after *Botha*), and apparently losing their nerve at the swift reaction of the Allied ships, broke off the bombardment, turned tail, and fled incontinently for their home ports—pursued by a force of about half their strength.

Then occurred one of those ironical incidents which causes one to question the existence of Cosmic Justice.

Admiral Bacon had justified much of his lack of offensive action on the grounds that, in the confusion of night battles, it was all too easy to mistake friend for foe and sink your own ships. Keyes had countered by pointing out that if clear, straightforward instructions were issued —and obeyed—and a simple code of identification lights used, these accidents could be avoided or at any rate reduced to a minimum.

At 4:35 A.M. *Botha* was racing up West Deep and

across the northeast end of Smal Bank, leading her division on a course converging with the escaping enemy. She sighted and engaged one of the bombarding groups of five German destroyers, and unfortunately was hit in her number two stokehold and a steam-pipe was cut, causing her speed to fall off. At the same time, she entered a smoke screen laid by the enemy, and when she emerged from the other side it was obvious that the Germans were drawing away. Immediately *Botha* turned to port to attack with torpedoes, and having got off two, continued to turn, as there suddenly appeared two German torpedo-boats hurrying after the destroyers. *Botha* rammed one M.T.B. (*A* 19) cutting her in two, and tried to turn in, even tighter, to do the same to the other. This was impossible, but the M.T.B. was raked from stem to stern by *Botha*'s fire, and left sinking.

By this time, *Botha* had turned in an arc of almost 180 degrees and re-entered the smoke screen—moreover, the German shell had cut some of her electric circuits as well as the steam-pipe, and her identification lights had been extinguished. It is easy, therefore, to sympathize with the Torpedo Officer of the *Capitaine Mehl*. He had seen his Flotilla Leader race forward into the smoke screen ahead, her guns blazing, her fighting lights visible: only a matter of seconds later, a darkened ship came past him, sailing upon an almost opposite course at an entirely different speed.

In the new spirit of aggressive action which had inspired the entire command since the new Admiral had arrived, the French officer yelled triumphantly and fired—and the torpedo hit *Botha* in her after stokehold and brought her to. By this time both the French captain and his torpedo officer had recognized their target—one can imagine their feelings.

*Botha* was towed back to Dunkirk by the *Morris,* with the French destroyers forming a protective screen, bringing up the rear like the mourners in a funeral cortège.

There is nothing so dispersive of gloom as action. The following day to counteract the despondency caused by this event, Keyes ordered the heavy monitor *Terror,* screened by a mixed destroyer flotilla, to carry out an immediate bombardment of Ostend Naval Base and basin, where our aircraft reported that the German destroyers had taken refuge after their scare. With Captain Douglas aboard to guide them to the buoy he had himself placed in position and to supervise the gunnery officer's use of his table and diagram, *Terror* fired 39 rounds, weighing in all 34 tons, at a range of 26,500 yards, before the enemy covered the target with smoke and Keyes ordered a cease-fire to avoid possible loss of life among the Belgian civilians.

Later, aerial photographs were taken by the planes of the Royal Naval Air Service Wing (also under the Dover Command) and they showed the very satisfactory state of affairs that all 39 shells had fallen within the boundaries of the Naval Base and basin.

A great improvement on 40 out of 185; although the range was greater, this time it was correct.

But the gunnery officers and crews were not the only people to profit from the work of the hydrographical officers. After some nights spent within small-arms range of the entrance to Ostend canal, Captain Douglas had established to within a yard the position of two large buoys—the Stroombank whistle buoy and a bell-buoy off Ostend beach, both of which had drifted far from their peacetime locations. Working with utmost accuracy in both directions from the Stroombank, he plotted a course which would bring the blockships on to the buoy, and another which would then take them from the buoy straight into the harbor entrance. With the help of Belgian pilots who had escaped to England, tides and local currents could be allowed for, and using Brock's calcium flares (another invention of this brilliant man still in use) a scheme was evolved whereby enemy defenses would be momentarily masked by smoke and shell-fire, and in those few precious minutes the blockships could be guided straight into the canal-mouth.

The method decided, attention could now be focused on the Ostend blockships and the men to sail in them.

From the six light cruisers made available by the Admiralty, four had now been earmarked for Zeebrugge—

*Vindictive, Thetis, Intrepid* and *Iphigenia*—and the remaining two, *Sirius* and *Brilliant,* remained for Ostend. The choice of commanding officers for both of these ships was made by Keyes, without reference to any other nominators. He wrote to Commander A. E. Godsal and offered him command of the *Brilliant* which was to lead, and then cast about in his mind for a captain for *Sirius*.

He turned once again to his Gallipoli experience, remembering an incident in Morto Bay.

The first landings on the peninsula had taken place on April 25, 1915, and on the 30th, Marshal Liman von Sanders received a peremptory order from Enver Pasha to 'drive the invaders into the sea.' The commander of the Turkish troops in the southern area, Colonel Sodenstern, received orders to assault the Allied line with every man available on the night of May 1st, and into the attack he flung 21 battalions of infantry—against a defensive line not more than three thousand yards long. Some of the bitter savagery of the attack is indicated by the incredible fact that orders were given for the Turkish rifles not to be loaded. "Attack the enemy with the bayonet and utterly destroy him," read the operational command. "We shall not retire one step; for if we do, our religion, our country, and our nation will perish."

It is not surprising that in places the Allied line cracked.

East of Sedd-el-Bahr, French Colonial troops retired to the beach in some confusion and were there met by a Lieutenant-Commander H. N. M. Hardy, the officer in charge of four British trawlers for the moment engaged in collecting and evacuating wounded. Hardy stopped the rout, found a Senegalese trumpeter among the demoralized and frightened soldiers, rallied them, and with the trumpeter beside him sounding the charge, led them back to the trenches they had just evacuated, handing them over to military command when the position had been stabilized.

Remembering this episode, Keyes sent for Hardy and appointed him to command *Sirius*.

With all the blockships selected and their captains appointed, Keyes now had to decide upon the exact manner in which the blocking was to be carried out.

At first, he was tempted to order the Zeebrugge block-ship captains to try to sail their ships through the gaunt-let of the first half-mile of the canal, ram the lock-gates if they were shut or enter the lock if they were open and sink themselves inside: surely one of the three should get through. But in the end, deep thought convinced him of the folly of this scheme and consultation with some local men who had escaped to England, persuaded him to take advantage of the silting-up which had taken place.

SECTION OF CANAL ENTRANCE—ZEEBRUGGE

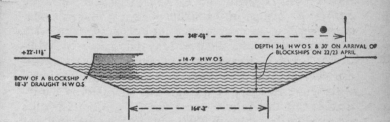

Aerial photographs revealed that under German occu-pation 'go slow' tactics on the part of the dredger crews, coupled with lack of spares for worn parts, had reduced efficiency to such a point that a complete silt-barrier had formed in one place, across which even the smallest sub-marines could not pass at low tide.

Both the sloping sides of the canal (see sketch) and the canal-bed itself, were paved with stone blocks. The blockships were a hundred yards along, and the minimum width which they must block was only 80 yards, but owing to the shelving canal-sides, the ships would not have this width to swing in, if they drew more than 18 feet 6 inches. Considerable care was essential therefore, in calculating the weight of concrete and rubble to be put aboard, and the positions it would occupy.

Since there was far more than an even chance that the blockships would be hit by shellfire, the concrete blocks could—in fact, must—be used to protect the vulnerable parts of the ship. But if too much was used the ship's draught would be too great for her to ride sufficiently far up the slope towards the canal-bank. Even when all auxiliary machinery was stripped, all copper and brass fittings removed (the enemy was known to be very short of these metals), armament stripped down until only the three foremost guns were left, and the bare minimum of coal for a return journey allowed for; even then, if all the vulnerable spots were adequately protected, the ships would have drawn too deep.

Eventually a compromise was worked out. Boilers and steering connexions were surrounded by mass concrete, which was also packed up into the bows above the waterline for protection and then in the stern to give balance. After consultations with salvage experts, bags of dry cement were placed in positions most calculated to prevent or hinder attempts to cut away parts of the ships, and empty spaces amidships were filled with rubble. The ships for blocking the canal at Ostend had a slightly greater margin of maneuver, for they could draw up to twenty-two feet and still effectively block the channel.

Each ship was provided with additional conning and steering positions fitted with duplicate controls and well protected with defensive mats, while half-inch-thick steel shields were fitted to the guns. Nine explosive charges were placed as deep down in each hull as possible, with firing keys in both control positions. In order to make the ships less conspicuous, the masts were taken out and smoke-making apparatus was fitted to increase what chances the crew had of getting away—always supposing many of them were in any condition to attempt to escape by the time the ships were securely bedded down.

In this connexion, Keyes had stressed the importance of the reliability and coolness under fire of the subordinate officers, chosen personally by each blockship captain, for—as he so cryptically phrased it—"the command might well pass rapidly."

Certainly, the chances of a safe return to England for the blockship crews appeared so slight as to be almost negligible—the odds were higher even for those of the submarines *C 1* and *C 3*. For this reason Keyes had insisted upon unmarried men, every one of whom should be a volunteer who knew the risks he was running. In

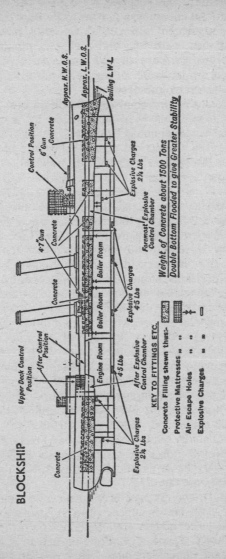

# BLOCKSHIP

Concrete

Explosive Charges 2½ Lbs

Upper Deck Control Position

After Control Position

After Explosive Control Chamber

4·5 Lbs

Engine Room

4·7 Gun

Concrete

Concrete

Boiler Room

Boiler Room

Explosive Charges 4·5 Lbs

Control Position

6" Gun

Concrete

Concrete

Explosive Charges 2½ Lbs

Foremost Explosive Control Chamber

Approx. H.W.O.S.

Approx. L.W.O.S.

Sailing L.W.L.

**KEY TO FITTINGS ETC.**

Concrete Filling shewn thus:-
Protective Mattresses   „   „
Air Escape Holes   „   „
Explosive Charges   „   „

Weight of Concrete about 1500 Tons
Double Bottom Flooded to give Greater Stability

Keyes's view, the risks run by the assault parties on the boardingships and the crews of the orthodox vessels taking part were no higher than those run every day by the infantry, locked now in the fiercest of the Somme Battles. In theory, therefore, there was no question of special volunteers for these positions: in practice, however, the supply of men wishing to take part in the operation vastly exceeded the demand, and there is good reason to believe that bribes were offered—but not accepted —in order to effect exchanges.

Another duty for which Keyes was willing to allow the volunteer principle to apply was that of manning the motor launches which were to follow the blockships into the canals and endeavor to take off the crews. There were five of these, one for each ship—although owing to the actual circumstances of the night, motor launches not in fact intended for the job did approach the Ostend blockships and help remove those aboard.

But most of the motor launches were to be engaged upon the all-important duty of laying and maintaining the smoke screens without which the first attack could never be delivered, nor the operation carried through without a disastrous casualty rate. The suicide mission has never held favor in British military thought, and despite Keyes's burning patriotism, the only life he would have been prepared to sacrifice deliberately was his own. An effective and controlled smoke screen was therefore considered a prime requisite, without which the operation would not take place.

There were also some protection duties for the launches to carry out, for it was thought that enemy E-boats and patrolcraft would be certain to try to interfere in some way. These must be dealt with by motor launches, while destroyers kept a wary eye open for heavier opposition which might conceivably be on its way down from the Heligoland Bight, or even just emerging from Bruges itself on normal patrol.

Coastal motor boats had also a large part to play. Faster than the M.L.s, and much lighter—lower deck belief had it that their hulls were composed of compressed paper—they were intended to be the first upon the scene, laying smoke screens as close inshore as possible; then when the M.L.s had closed up, C.M.B. units were to split up and carry out a variety of tasks from endeavoring to seek out enemy destroyers moored to the inner side of the Mole and torpedo them, to placing Brock's calcium buoys in position to guide in the Ostend blockships.

Altogether, there were 18 C.M.B.s in the Dover squadron and six available at Dunkirk, and for the purposes of the operation those which were to accompany the Zeebrugge assault came under the command of Lieutenant A. E. P. Welman, R.N. This young man, who had already commanded the C.M.B. flotilla at Dover for nearly a year, was just 24—yet so assured and impressive was his personality that Keyes had not the faintest hesitation in confirming him in full operational control of these vital small craft.

By now the 4th Battalion of the Royal Marines had been formed at Dover. On King's Down the shape of the Mole had been marked out and was vigorously attacked day and night from every angle, in the carefully propagated belief that it represented a fortified post just behind enemy lines in France. The battalion was commanded by Acting Lieutenant-Colonel B. H. Elliot, an officer in the tradition of the Sea Regiment, whose forebears had served with it since 1716. Elliot had already won a D.S.O. in Serbia, when, after the fall of Belgrade, he rallied the survivors of his force and led them on foot across the entire width of that mountainous and bandit-ridden country.

Two hundred Bluejackets formed the Naval assault parties, some of whom, having served for three years in the Naval Brigade or with the Royal Naval siege guns in front of Dunkirk, had seen more trench fighting than many an infantryman. However, all were now given a course in fighting with bomb and bayonet, Lewis gun and rifle.

Fifty Bluejackets from the Grand Fleet under command of Lieutenant C. Dickinson received specialist instruction in demolitions; models and drawings of the guns, dredgers, and cranes which were known to exist had been made, and the men were taught exactly how much explosive would be needed to destroy each object, and where to place it.

All Naval assault personnel came under command of Captain H. C. Halahan, R.N., who had previously commanded the siege guns. Keyes had approached him, asking for names of men he could recommend to take part in a hazardous enterprise, and he duly sent in the list of names with a covering letter which ended:

"May I say that if the operation for which you said you might want these men is eventually undertaken, I should very much like to take part in it. I would willingly accept the same conditions, viz., that I should not expect to come back."

Since it was impossible for all these men to be accommodated in either the *Vindictive* or the refitting blockships, Keyes requisitioned H.M.S. *Hindustan,* a paid-off battleship which was lying at Chatham with a skeleton crew, and the new arrivals took up quarters on board her.

The word was spreading now, despite the strictest security precautions which could be enforced, and from all branches of the Navy the lone wolves were coming in; men of the breed who know instinctively when plans for unorthodox warfare are in the air, the individuals, the rebels, the men of fire.

E. Harrington Edwards was one of these, a bearded warrior who had lost an eye at Gallipoli, since been badly wounded with the Naval Brigade in France and who was to end the war in North Russia where he managed to collect yet another wound. The Reverend C. Peshall was another, an international rugby player who was recommended to Keyes on the grounds that if the situation became critical, he could be relied upon to forget his collar and join an assault or defense group as a highly efficient fighting member. De Berry was there and Bamford of the R.M.L.I.—and Dallas Brooks and Finch of the Blue Marines: one name famous in the Corps already, one to become a legend.

Carpenter and Bradford, McKenzie and Dean, the Sandford brothers; Petty Officer Youlton who burnt off his boots—and Lake who was to juggle with red-hot Mills bombs.

A gallant band—whose spirit had come down to them from Drake and Hawkins, and which was to burn so brightly again in the Baders, the Gibsons, the David Stirlings and the Durnford-Slaters of World War II. It is fortunate for Britain that in peacetime this spirit only sleeps —and does not die.

But what of the man who led them?

He had taken command at Dover on January 1st. By the end of March, he had changed the barring of the Dover Straits from a hollow mockery to a hard, triumphant reality; he had reorganized the system of coastal bombardment until it was effective; he had inspired the invention and use of a smoke screen which for the first time equalled that of the enemy—and he had organized, practically from scratch, the first amphibious assault on a hostile and defended coast ever to be launched from British shores since oak and cannonball had been replaced by steel plate and explosive shell: this after senior officers had been considering for four years without producing a workable plan.

One gains the impression of almost transatlantic hustle, yet the photograph taken at this time shows no sign of any aggressive forcefulness. Sincerity is there, and a tiredness around the eyes which speaks, not of boredom or weariness of character, but of a willing acceptance of the strains of deep responsibility. But of assertiveness there is no trace. He was present at a wedding years afterwards, and another guest telling of his presence there, has said: "I was a young girl of just fourteen, and so terribly excited at the prospect of meeting Sir Roger that I thought I would be too shy, and make an awful *gaucherie*. But when I met him, he was the one who was shy— so shy that I felt positively protective, and did everything I could to keep other people from worrying him. I honestly believe he was grateful."

He probably was—the diffidence of character is noticeable—but where is the will power which must have existed? Some of the answer can be seen in another photograph, taken in 1915 on board the *Triad* during the Gallipoli campaign. Admiral De Robeck is in the photograph with him—and General Sir Ian Hamilton and Major-General Braithwaite—and there is a grimness about Keyes's mouth and eyes which tells of his reaction to the temporizing and irresolution which he suspected in other members of the group. This was the expression on his face, one feels, when he grappled with inertia at the Admiralty and complacency at Dover; with inefficiency among the patrol craft and ill luck among the destroyers. The necessary driving force is there after all.

Another photograph, another trait—and one which perhaps explains the combination of shyness and power, clear-sightedness and utter lack of cynicism.

It is a photograph taken by the Queen of the Belgians at La Panne in August, 1918, and Sir Roger Keyes stands proudly beside the King whom he served so devotedly. There is no doubt about the pride and happiness which Keyes felt at the moment, for his smile is one of pure delight and he looks even more like an engaging schoolboy than usual—a schoolboy, moreover, who could quite easily be cheeky, but who for the moment is immensely pleased with the world in general and himself in particular.

He never lost a boyish simplicity and naturalness.

Some time in the late 1940's an old retired petty officer, his face red with a combination of sincerity and embarrassment, sought out Keyes's biographer and said, "I've been thinking about that book, sir, that book you said you were writing about Lord Keyes. There's one particular thing I should like you to say in it, sir. Will you please say how much we all loved him."

Now that they knew the object of the expedition, members of the sailing crews came forward to ask that they be left aboard, and the blockships steam to their final destination fully manned. When this request was refused, a certain truculence manifested itself and the spirit aboard, if not actually mutinous, verged upon the cheerfully defiant.

In the meantime, Keyes had concluded that his first intention—to command the operation from the decks of the *Vindictive*—was impracticable, as he must be free to move around and ensure that the various separate phases were all going well. He therefore decided to fly his flag in the fast destroyer *Warwick* (Commander Victor Campbell) and thus put himself in a rather awkward position.

Commander Carpenter had begged for a position aboard *Vindictive,* and in view of his immense contribution towards the planning of the operation combined with his experience and known ability as a navigating officer, Keyes had readily acceded to his request and promised that he should have the position of flag captain. There could be no objection whatsoever to a comparatively junior commander commanding *Vindictive* under the aegis and flag of a vice-admiral on board, but there would be loud and justifiable criticism if the same junior commander had complete charge of the largest and in some ways most important ship of the fleet.

Even if the Admiralty were willing to promote Carpenter (local, acting, unpaid), Captain Halahan would be aboard with his Bluejacket assault force, and nothing could affect his seniority as a captain—which would automatically make him senior executive officer on the ship. At first, Keyes attempted to abide by regulation and precedent, and he told Carpenter that circumstances had combined against them and that he must withdraw his promise.

Carpenter understood, sympathized with Keyes and nobly agreed that there was no alternative—but his generosity was the last straw which broke Keyes's already hesitant decision. Always prone to see himself in another's predicament, Keyes knew how heartbroken Carpenter must be feeling, called in Halahan and laid down exact responsibilities for each of them, in a situation which proved workable but nevertheless remained highly irregular.

Carpenter was to con the ship and lay her alongside the Mole but he had no authority whatsoever over the boarding parties or assault crews who sailed on his ship, and within reason he was to accede to Captain Halahan's requests in regard to factors of time and position. *Daffodil* would now, of course, come under Carpenter's orders, and finally—with the feeling that if success came the Admiralty wouldn't cavil, and if all failed the extra disapprobation would be but a drop in the ocean—Keyes told Carpenter to add another stripe and, on his own personal authority, had his promotion to Acting Captain published in orders.

Commodore Hubert Lynes had commanded the Dunkirk detachment of the Dover Command under Admiral Bacon, and Keyes had been relieved to find that there was no necessity whatever to make a change. Commodore Lynes was efficient, open-minded and possessed of considerable charm—a most valuable attribute in his dealings with Frenchmen on French soil under English command. As Keyes could not take charge of both the Zeebrugge and Ostend operations (there is a difference of only forty minutes between high water at these two ports, so the two operations would be simultaneous), he placed command of the western attack in Lynes's hands without reserve and with a complete confidence which ensured Lynes's most heartfelt cooperation.

And now they waited, all of them, from the rawest, most newly-joined deckhand to Keyes himself, in an atmosphere of cool, but lively, anticipation.

In addition, Admiral Tyrwhitt waited at Harwich for the word which would send his destroyer force out to cover the northern approaches and a possible attack from the Heligoland Bight: the pilots of the Handley-Page bombers of the 63rd Wing at Guston aerodrome waited for the time when they would fly out to unload their bombs above the enemy gun-positions. At Dunkirk, the monitor captains checked their ammunition and hoped that the combination of Douglas's buoys and Altham's gyro-director would prove as effective at night as it had during the afternoon of March 22nd.

And although he may have been unaware of it, three people moved closer to Keyes to try to shield him from unbearable strain; his wife, his lifelong friend, and his coxswain.

Keyes had now been married for twelve years and was already the father of two daughters and the son who was to win the Victoria Cross and imperishable fame in the raid on Rommel's headquarters, 23 years later in the deserts of North Africa. They were all with him at Dover, and the feelings experienced by his wife as she watched the preparations, are best left to the imagination; indeed they must be, for in the true tradition of service wives, she kept her innermost misgivings to herself, and faced the world—and especially her husband—with a cheerful and dauntless courage which was a soothing balm to Keyes's occasionally bruised spirit and an inspiration to his faith.

Now she listened to his troubles, left him to his occasional deep, impenetrable silences, and prayed for his safety and some measure of success in his efforts, which might serve to placate the forces which drove him on.

In all this she had the heartfelt cooperation of two men.

Since January 13th, when Captain Tomkinson came south from the Grand Fleet to take up his invariable position by the side of his immediate superior and greatest friend, he had worked day and night on the details of the operation. Now that these details were completed, he could concentrate once more upon what had become his principal task in life—to protect Keyes from the effects of his own spirit and other men's jealousy.

Wilfred Tomkinson had been been Keyes's first lieutenant in the 300-ton destroyer *Fame* during the China War, and together they had captured four Chinese destroyers in a cutting-out operation worthy of Pellew, blown up the powder magazine of a Boxer fort, curbed riots on the Kowloon peninsula, and it was Tomkinson who had looked after *Fame* while Keyes was off, earning his first right to a place in history by sliding through the sluice-gates of the Pekin Legation at the head of the relieving force.

Since Keyes had reached the necessary authority to hold any sway in Naval appointments, he had always endeavored to have his old friend by his side; thus eight years later, upon his first captain's appointment, he tried to get Tomkinson once again as his first lieutenant; when he was Inspecting Captain of submarines, we find Commander Tomkinson with a flotilla leader, and upon the outbreak of war, Tomkinson was given command of the fast destroyer *Lurcher* in which Commodore Keyes flew his broad-pendant during the actions of both Heligoland Bight and Dogger Bank.

They were parted during the Gallipoli campaign, but Keyes had hardly returned to the Grand Fleet at Scapa Flow and hoisted his Rear-Admiral's flag on the *Colossus,* when her captain, Dudley Pound, was appointed to the Admiralty (where he afterwards became First Sea Lord) —and Captain Tomkinson arrived to take his place. Six months later Tomkinson was at Dover, nominally as destroyer fleet captain, in reality once again his friend's most trusted aide.

If there seems to readers of the works of Mr. C. S. Forester, something of the Hornblower-Bush tradition in all this, then they will recognize with delight another permanent feature of Keyes's seagoing life. In the cutting-out operation referred to above, it had been necessary for one of the crew of *Fame* to leap aboard the leading enemy destroyer, and ignoring the actions of both Chinese and his own shipmates, hook a hawser and ship's anchor around the enemy mast. From the volunteers who stepped forward (the entire deck crew) Keyes chose a young able seaman named Henry Brady, and from that moment until the end of Keyes's seagoing career, Brady was his coxswain.

So these three watched and waited—Mrs. Keyes at home, Tomkinson and Brady at headquarters and at sea; and the man who was the center of their world—and now the focus of nearly a thousand other men's worlds too —listened to the sounds of the wind and the waves, read

70

the reports of the fierce action on the Western Front, and prayed to the fighting seaman's God, for a chance to emulate his heroes and serve his Country and his King.

Slowly but inexorably, time passed and the days of the dark period arrived.

April the 9th and 10th went by with high winds and too-rough seas, and on the 11th Sir Douglas Haig—a man of few words—thought fit to awaken the nation to the terrible bitterness of the Somme battle then being fought by issuing the following Order of the Day:

"With our backs to the wall, and believing in the justice of our cause, each one of us must fight on to the end. The safety of our homes and the freedom of mankind depend alike upon the conduct of each one of us at this critical moment."

Keyes read this in the morning, and shortly afterwards the meteorological report for the day was brought in. It was the most suitable so far—yet one can sense in Keyes's reports and actions that day, that he felt intuitively that the time was not yet. Nevertheless, spurred on by the Army Commander's words, he issued the preparatory signal for the operation to commence. With a smoothness which paid high tribute to the staff work of Carpenter and Tomkinson, the forces moved towards their appointed places.

Captain Douglas and Lieutenant-Commander Haselfoot were the first away, Douglas joining the 15-inch monitors *Erebus* and *Terror* to guide them to the Zeebrugge bombarding positions off the Dutch coast, and Haselfoot joining a small monitor guarded by destroyers, to lay the essential guide buoys.

Commodore Boyle (Chief of Staff, Dover Patrol), had managed to secure himself a place in the operation despite his other responsibilities, and hoisted his broad pendant in the light cruiser *Attentive*. He left Dover in the early afternoon, in company with the flotilla leader *Scott* and three destroyers. Two of the attendant craft remained behind at 'D' buoy and one at 'C', while Boyle himself proceeded to 'G' buoy, marking a point in the

Belgian coast minefield which had been carefully but inconspicuously cleared to let the expedition through.

From this point he was carefully to note the direction and force of the wind, and report on it to Keyes in the approaching squadron by means of a flashing light passed through the craft he had left behind him. Under no circumstances would this signal-light be answered, and strict wireless silence was imposed upon everyone, except for single code words which would be sent out from *Warwick* on Keyes's instructions only, and which would signify either successful stages, or changes of plan.

At 4 P.M., the blockships, the *Vindictive* and the ferryboats up in the Swin got under way and sailed down to join their escorting armada from Dover at a point seven miles east of Ramsgate. At 7:30 P.M., the entire squadron formed up and set out—nearly a thousand men with nerves tightened to a point of exhilaration, and with the light, expanding fullness of heart which comes to eager men before battle. There were, however, exceptions to this mood of confidence—Keyes and the men immediately around him, by now infected by his secret uncertainty.

"My thoughts turned constantly to the assault on Santa Cruz in the Island of Tenerife in July, 1797, when Nelson's impatient ardor impelled him to undertake a hazard, foredoomed by the state of the weather," Keyes wrote later. "All went well for a time, such wind as there was blew gently towards the Belgian coast, and I prayed that it would continue to do so—at any rate until we got to grips with the enemy—and that if it did not, that I would have the moral courage to break off the operation and await a more favorable opportunity."

What more favorable opportunity? And even if another was presented, would Keyes be permitted to take it? This was the question which must have weighed so heavily on his mind. 76 vessels had left 'A' buoy, and another 60 ships were at sea as flank screen, Ostend force or bombarding monitors. It was strongly arguable that they could not all have left harbor without the enemy's gaining some knowledge of it—and of the objective. The Admiralty could hardly be blamed if they refused to allow him to

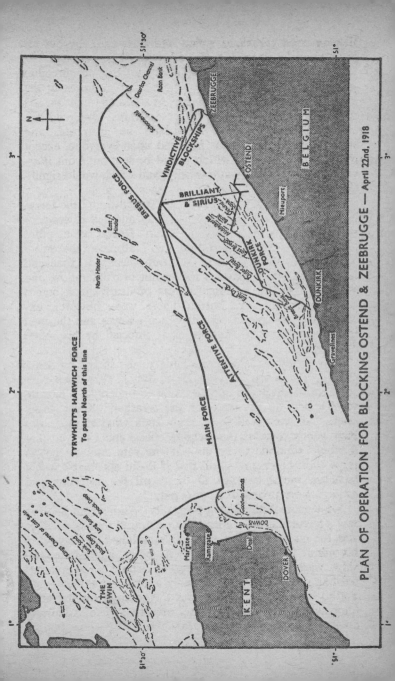

PLAN OF OPERATION FOR BLOCKING OSTEND & ZEEBRUGGE — April 22nd, 1918

risk men and ships in a second attempt at an exploit dangerous enough with everything in its favor, but triply so after an abortive sortie in which the whole design of the attack might well have been revealed to some alert enemy agent in the vicinity.

And now, every yard nearer they steamed to their objective, the smaller would be that chance of a second opportunity if Keyes was forced to call a halt and return the squadron to base.

At 11 P.M. 'C' buoy was reached, 35 miles from Zeebrugge, and the wind report was still favorable. Keyes sent out the code word signifying to the detached vessels that the program would be adhered to, and half an hour later the bombers were over Zeebrugge and Ostend, and the night was shaken with the crump of bombs and lit by the soaring 'flaming onions' of the German antiaircraft defenses.

Then at twelve-thirty, when the squadron had reached 'D' buoy and had slowed for the removal of the blockship crews, the wind dropped. For a few minutes, watched by a hundred anxious eyes, immobile clouds patched the sky; on the decks below, malicious gusts chased each other playfully around the compass—and died.

Slowly, inexorably, the clouds began to move northwards—away from the coast. So would the smoke screens now, and the attacking ships would be revealed long before they could close with the waiting enemy.

There was such overwhelming temptation to go on and risk it.

Everyone was keyed up to the battle—the men were trained to a hair, the officers bursting with eagerness to put into concrete effect all their planning, all their hopes and dreams of the past few weeks.

Surely, with the whole expedition poised so exquisitely for the attack, by its very momentum it would sweep away the extra difficulties created by the fickle wind, and the enemy would go down before the spirit and *élan* of the attackers?

It was all so near—so almost within their grasp.

If they went on to a glorious success, that would be fine but if they failed—well Keyes would at least be there with them in the battle, not like some poor Army general, forced to remain miles back from the front line in safety and horrid security. Keyes would fail with them, and quite easily might not live to face the opprobrium of failure.

A tempting thought that—but possibly the one which decided him, for he would never seek exculpation, even in death.

At 12:35, Keyes looked quickly around the group of officers on the bridge with him, glanced once more at the sky, sighed, and spoke quietly to the officer beside him. Seconds later, one word went out over the radio—and Captain Carpenter was faced with the task of turning a convoy of 75 vessels on a pitch-black night without navigation lights.

*Warwick* stopped engines and lay south of the main force, while Keyes stared into the blackness of the night which shrouded his squadron, now executing as difficult a maneuver as any in the history of the Royal Navy. What made the feat even more difficult was the fact that *Iris* and *Daffodil* had been found to be bad sailors on a long voyage, and it was therefore decided to tow them astern of *Vindictive*—and also, in order to conserve the fuel and engine lives of the C.M.B.s, the two explosive-packed submarines, and Sandford's picket-boat, the same decision had been taken regarding them. This meant that every large ship towed something—and Carpenter, in addition to his responsibility for the entire squadron, now had to turn *Vindictive* with two ferryboats and a C.M.B. tied on behind.

And yet it was done—with trifling loss. For the actual turn, the C.M.B.s had started up their engines, and one, unable to keep her tow-rope taut, was cut down and sunk—fortunately with no loss of life. More important was the fact that Keyes was satisfied that during the reversal, no lights could have been seen by the enemy, for the smaller craft were not fitted with wireless and the order to turn had been flashed to them by signal-lamp.

Gradually the roar of the C.M.B.s' engines became a distant rumble, the thick hiss of disturbed water died away, the fascinating, frightening presence of an invisible

75

fleet receded. Keyes gave orders for *Warwick* to get under way, but before they left, they were reminded of the power they challenged. Four heavy shells suddenly screamed out towards them and pitched with astonishing accuracy into the water 200 yards away, sending up spouts of water to twice the height of *Warwick's* mast.

The enemy was alert—and would be possibly more so in the future. Moreover, they were apparently in possession of some form of sound or wireless ranging—of which nothing was known.


Satisfied that none of his vessels were still to the southward, Keyes gave orders for *Warwick* to proceed straight to the Swin, and upon arrival he went aboard each ship and spoke to the men. The atmosphere was far from pleasant—Keyes had expected that—but his sincerity was patent and by now he had one saving factor to help him. By the time he spoke to the men, his decision had been proved correct—at daylight, the wind was blowing freshly from the south. By turning back a disaster had been averted.

He told them so and swore before heaven that he would lead them on to a glorious success, not an heroic failure. The men were reassured and cheered him to the echo.

Feeling much better, Keyes returned to Dover and telephoned Commodore Lynes at Dunkirk. Lynes reported that he had not stopped the monitor bombardment—there was no harm in that—and that the destroyers and small craft, with one exception, had withdrawn without exposing themselves to the enemy. However, *C.M.B. 33* had not returned—and as yet Lynes could offer no explanation why.

He never did produce an explanation, and this was as well, for *C.M.B. 33* had gone aground on the shoals near the Ostend canal-mouth, and the young officer in command had disobeyed explicit instructions in that he had taken with him into the danger area sufficient written material for the enemy to deduce that we had planned an attack on Ostend. By use of a little imagination, they would also undoubtedly have been able to guess that our designs on the Belgian coast were not confined to that area alone.

However, all this was not known until much later.

Their Lordships did not act at once.

During the rest of April 12th, Keyes sifted through the reports of the night's events, made note of possible adjustments in the program—and waited. On the morning of the 13th, the wind was within the prescribed limits, and with a feeling that he was to a certain extent on borrowed time, Keyes sent out the preparatory signal.

However, two hours after the Swin Force had actually got under way and was steaming down towards the Goodwins, the wind freshened almost to gale force and once more the cancellation signal went out. It was the last night of the April dark period.

Keyes knew what would happen now—it only remained to see when.

The blow fell the following day.

Sir Rosslyn Wemyss arrived at Dover during the forenoon and if Keyes had still any doubts as to Their Lordships' reaction, they must have been immediately dispelled by the forced air of Sir Rosslyn's invariable urbanity. The First Sea Lord started by commiserating with Keyes on his bad luck, and endeavored to sugar this pill by telling him—rightly—how admirable had been Keyes's decision to withdraw in the circumstances. Then, through the preliminary arguments of loss of surprise element, loss of initial moral stimulus, impossibility of keeping the men cooped up on board ship, he led up to the news that it had been decided to disband the force and abandon the expedition.

"It will," he said, "be at least three weeks before the next dark period will allow. . . ."

Keyes, who had sat up most of the night rehearsing smooth blandishments and cogent pleas, forgot his rhetoric in the fierce heat of desperation. "Why wait three weeks? I want to try again in nine or ten days!"

Sir Rosslyn stared. One can visualize the pause, the wiped eyeglass, the mouth pouted in surprise.

"But," he said, "it will be full moon then, and you have always stipulated a dark night with no moon."

"No, no! I always wanted a full moon!" announced Keyes outrageously, and then, borne passionately along on a wave of transparent fabrication which bore no relation at all to recorded fact, continued—"but I couldn't wait for one. Please go back and tell the Board that you approve of my carrying out the attack in the next period when high tide occurs about midnight!"

He must have looked like an earnest—but so engaging—schoolboy. Wemyss, after staring at him open-mouthed for a few seconds, burst into laughter.

"Roger," he said, "what a deuced liar you are!"

But Keyes had won—the operation was on again.

# 5

THE WEEK that followed was dreadful for everybody. At Keyes's suggestion and with the full co-operation of the Naval Staff, spurred on by Sir Rosslyn, the battle-ship *Dominion* was sent to the Swin, and the cramped conditions on the *Hindustan* immediately relieved as the assault parties expanded to fill the living-quarters of both ships. Cooks, mess-waiters and stores arrived in an attempt to alleviate the physical aspect of the situation —but in a retreat from unfulfilled excitement it is the mind that suffers most.

A thousand men had been brought to a peak of phys-ical and nervous excellence: now they were held in cir-cumstances which suggested living in a vacuum. They could neither send nor receive mail, they were out of sight of land but not moving, and attempts to resume training had the attraction of a twice-cooked dinner.

In his office at Dover, Keyes dealt with the day-to-day administration of his command, conferred with his senior officers, and saw that all possible precautions against leakage of information were taken; when busy with these duties his mind could ignore some of the waiting strain, and his nerves relax. But the pressure built up—he was not busy all the time and there were periods when his mental horizon seemed bounded by the Mole and his spirit crushed by its weight. "The week that fol-lowed," he wrote later, "was one of the most trying I have ever spent in my life."

In view of the experiences of the abortive approach to the target there were some minor changes of plan—for instance, the gap in the minefield was widened at the sug-gestion of Commodore Lynes, and two flashing Aga buoys (further products of Wing-Commander Brock's fertile genius) were positioned to mark the limits be-tween which the ships must pass. Alterations in timing took place too; 'M' buoy was eliminated and Zero

Hour was fixed at the moment of passing 'G' buoy—now located between the Aga buoys.

There were also changes of personnel, mostly unimportant, but one caused by a stroke of cruel luck which removed one of the chief figures of the days of preparation just before he would have reaped his reward. After laboring so long and so industriously upon the fitting of the blockships, Lieutenant Ivan Franks developed severe internal pains during the wait in the Swin. One can imagine the gnawing anxiety with which the young officer compared the slow creep of time towards the first possible state of tide for the attack, with the growing fire in his abdomen—which crisis would arrive first? In agony he forced himself hour after hour to ignore the symptoms—to keep himself standing up just long enough to sail for Belgium. But it was not to be—on the third day after the return to the Swin, he collapsed and was rushed to Chatham Hospital with acute appendicitis.

Even in the depths of his disappointment, however, his thoughts remained with his crew and his command. Just before the stretcher-bearers carried him away, he managed to scribble a note to Keyes, imploring him to appoint his friend and chosen second-in-command, Lieutenant E. W. Billyard-Leake, in his place.

This was by no means a light request, for there is considerable difference between the position and responsibilities of a ship's captain, and those of even the most senior of his subordinate officers. The captain is on a pinnacle, his officers inhabit a sloping plateau well below; promotion to ultimate authority is by no means automatic. Billyard-Leake at this time moreover, was a lieutenant of only a year's standing and an extremely youthful one at that—younger even than that presiding genius of the C.M.B.s, Lieutenant Welman.

However, hard on the heels of Ivan Franks's request came another couched in exactly similar terms, this time bearing the signatures of every man of *Iphigenia's* crew from junior rating to navigating officer. In the face of such unanimity Keyes agreed, and Billyard-Leake took command. He was, at the time, within weeks of his 22nd birthday.

Altogether there were 22 vacancies caused by sickness during the wait in the Swin, with the usual results when demand exceeds supply; a type of black market in chances to join the operation arose among the crews of *Hindustan* and *Dominion*. Several requests were made to be allowed to drop rank. The keenest bidding was for positions on the blockships, and it seems to have been generally accepted that while a genuine claim to sail with the expedition was preferable, if none existed, then it was excusable tactics to smuggle aboard somehow and hope to remain unnoticed until after sailing-time.

As a result, when the blockships and assault craft left Dover they carried a full complement of such improbable people as sick berth attendants and mess-waiters, officers' servants and cooks, and there were even some members of the civilian victualling firm aboard *Vindictive*. When Keyes found an officer aboard her whom he knew quite well had no right to be there, he was informed rather sheepishly that as some of the officer's kit seemed to have been put aboard, the officer thought he'd better come along to look after it. It is typical of the spirit of both the enterprise and its leader that the officer stayed.

Grudgingly the hours passed, until eventually the morning of the first possible day of the new high tide period arrived. It was April 22nd, and in the accounts of Keyes's actions can be felt, first an easy, faintly-surprised wonderment, then acceptance hardening as the hours passed to a firm conviction. The weather report was not bad but it was by no means ideal, for the essential northerly wind was unsteady and visibility promised to be extreme, even for a time of bright moonlight.

Yet there was none of the tense uncertainty which had accompanied the far better conditions on April 11th. Having sent off the preparatory and the executive signals setting the whole operation in train for the third time, Keyes spent the remaining hours ashore in an atmosphere of calm, relaxed confidence which puzzed his staff. Surprised at his early decision and aware that the passing hours brought no appreciable improvement in the weather, they fully expected another cancellation.

But Keyes had no doubts—no deep, fundamental

doubts anyway—and empirical ones raised by mutable factors of weather were reduced to naught by his wife's words as they walked together down to the harbor just before sailing.

"Tomorrow," said Mrs. Keyes, "is St. George's Day. . . ."

And in this revelation Keyes's intuition, his simple sailor's faith—his whole attitude to life, creed and country—crystallized into a certainty that now was the time. His hour had struck.

"St. George," continued Mrs. Keyes firmly, "can be trusted to bring good fortune to England!"

It was the needed incalculable—the irrational tenth as Lawrence called it. In a mood of exaltation and high purpose, Keyes went aboard *Warwick* to lead the small craft out and join the main force at 'A' buoy. The squadron sailed at 5 P.M. Shortly before dusk, he sent out by semaphore as simple a battle signal as any in history:

"St. George for England."

It was to become a famous signal in the Royal Navy, but its immediate result was not altogether happy. Aboard *Vindictive,* Commander Carpenter was in a mood of confident high spirits quite different from the almost mystical faith which uplifted Keyes.

"May we give the dragon's tail a damned good twist!" Carpenter signalled back, which—as Keyes sorrowfully recorded—"was very apt and to the point, but did not fit in with my mood at the moment."

Once again, *Vindictive* led the van.

*Warwick* took station well ahead of the starboard column, led by the flotilla leader *Phoebe,* and from this position Keyes was able to keep the main striking-force of assault and blockships under close observation. Light aircraft flew overhead while daylight lasted, both to keep off enemy spotting planes who could wreck the enterprise by robbing it of its essential element of surprise, and also to give warning of any approaching surface-craft. Visibility decreased slightly before dusk, and clouds forming overhead gave rise to fears that the sea might get up and swamp the C.M.B.s, but after darkness fell, the clouds thinned and the rising moon shed a silver radiance over the water.

The horizon was clearly visible, as were even the smallest ships at the tail of the convoy, but there was justification for faith in England's patron saint after all, for gradually a mist formed, thickened, and objects more than a mile away faded into obscurity. Later rain fell coldly—but helpfully.

On the ships, men completed the grisly last-minute preparations before action. The surgeon's paraphernalia was laid out, stretcher-parties took up inconspicuous but strategic positions, first-aid dressings were made available for all, bundles of them being piled in odd corners around the decks. Candle lamps were placed alongside electric bulbs; hoses drenched woodwork and matting, and the glinting stacks of ammunition grew alongside the guns and mortars. Encompassing all was the tension of men readying themselves for battle: the creak of webbing, the clink of weapons, the sudden barking cough instantly suppressed, the grimmer voices and the deep, deafening silences among the waiting men underlined by the purposeful swearing of those fortunate enough to be busy.

In a fleet of that size and containing a high proportion of outdated craft, mechanical breakdowns could be expected. Eighteen miles out from Dover, *C.M.B. 35A* fouled her propellers and from their respective decks the crews of her sister-ships watched her drop behind, commenting between them with sympathy or jibes according to nature. They all reckoned, however, without the determination of Lieutenant E. E. Hill who commanded the vessel. Hailing a nearby drifter, he bullied or cajoled her captain into towing him straightway back to Dover. Within half an hour of arrival, his craft was hoisted out of the water and half the available dockyard staff were working like blacks to free his jammed propellers and repair secondary damage. At 9:40 P.M. *C.M.B. 35A* again cleared Dover harbor, and with a fine disregard of such dangers as excessive fuel consumption or unknown minefields, sped like an arrow across to Zeebrugge, arriving in time to take up her smoke patrol off the Mole.

By a curious accident the motor launch detailed to remove the surplus steaming-crew from *Intrepid* also broke down, so Bonham Carter had a crew of 87 instead of 54, to help him take his command into the canal mouth. An air of jaunty self-satisfaction was noticeable among the men who thus avoided removal, becoming more marked during the short wait at 'D' buoy when other motor launches went past bearing a few disconsolate figures from *Thetis* and *Iphigenia*. Even from these ships however, the numbers removed were not as high as they should have been, for when the time came for the masters-at-arms to parade the excess steaming-crews and see them over the side, the decks became unaccountably deserted.

"Oh no, Chief," a stoker generously assured his immediate superior, ten minutes after the fleet had resumed course. "We ain't blaming you at all—as you 'ave so often told us, you're a busy man. It's h'entirely our own fault we got left be'ind!"

He gazed blandly back at the stony face before him.

"Pity, ain't it?" he said, thumbing back the catch of a service rifle. "But as I'm 'ere—got any spare ammo?"

While the few unfortunates who had been unsuccessful in their attempts to remain with the expedition were being transferred to the minesweeper *Lingfield,* the C.M.B.s were slipped from tow. In *Vindictive,* advantage was taken of both the temporary lull and the presence of the extra cooks. Hot soup was issued to the men, while cocoa made to the correct Naval specification (unaided, the spoon must stand upright) made its appearance on the bridge.

Then with *Iris, Daffodil*, the submarines *C 1* and *C 3* and their attendant picket-boat all still in tow, the convoy started off again. They reached and passed between the Aga buoys marking the gap in the minefield—where Commodore Boyle in *Attentive* was still faithfully reporting the northerly breeze, the cloud ceiling, the rising chop— exactly on time. This was 'G' position and the time was 10:30 P.M.—'X' hour.

Fifteen miles and ninety minutes to go.

*Brilliant, Sirius,* two destroyers, and two C.M.B.s now altered course and departed for Ostend, while *Warwick*

84

drew out a mile ahead of the main force with L Unit (Destroyers *Phoebe* and *North Star*) astern, and F Unit (*Whirlwind* and *Myngs*) to port—the whole flotilla charged with the duty of driving off enemy ships which might emerge either from behind the Mole or from the harbor of Blankenberghe, some four miles to westward.

The allocated duties for *Phoebe* and *North Star* were to shepherd the assault ships into position and then to form an outer guard for the blockships, and Keyes decided to keep *Warwick* in a position to drive off any torpedo attacks which the enemy might try from the seaward side of the Mole. If German units did manage to reach the open sea, the position of the assault craft would be precarious indeed—anchored to the side of the Mole, unmaneuverable and completely defenseless on the seaboard side, three well-placed torpedoes could sink them all and result in the total loss of the Royal Marine contingent, the Bluejacket assault parties and the naval crews.

By now the night was black, and the thin rain which had started falling during the wait at 'D' buoy was thickening. As a result there was no sign of the air bombardment which should have commenced an hour earlier. Bombarding fire from the monitors *Erebus* and *Terror* was delayed also, due to low visibility. However, this commenced fifteen minutes later when Captain Douglas picked up the Oost Gat light, accurately marking the limits of Dutch territorial waters.

At 11:10 P.M. the first units went ahead on the final leg which would close the enemy.

Units A and B, consisting of three C.M.B.s, forged ahead at full speed towards positions from which they would lay smoke across the entire front of the advance; ten minutes later, Unit C (*C.M.B. 16A*) detached herself and raced south towards Blankenberghe harbor, where she spent the ensuing hours laying and renewing smoke floats, and then lurking behind the resultant clouds in wait for enemy craft to emerge and offer targets for her torpedo tubes.

All the C.M.B.s were up with the leading destroyers now, and the heavier M.L.s were closing up too, leaving only the assault craft, the blockships and their special attendant small craft in the rear. At 11:20 P.M. Unit E (*C.M.B. 28A*) forged ahead towards an inshore position where she would begin laying the first smoke screens actually inside the sweep of the Mole, and the M.L.s of Unit I trudged after her in support. Perceptibly now, the pace was quickening as the attackers approached their individual targets; nerves tightened and hearts thumped. There was as yet no response from the enemy.

At 11:30 P.M. *Warwick,* ten minutes ahead of the assault ships, steamed past an occulting light buoy five miles northwest of Zeebrugge Mole; parallel with her, Lieutenant Hill was roaring across the last minefields on his way into position from Dover. Like ants attacking a rotten apple, the head of the convoy split into component strands and led out towards the battle positions.

The destroyer screens broke apart and fanned out; *C.M.B.s 22B* and *23B* of Unit V with the youthful Lieutenant Welman in command sped forward to lay smoke directly under the barrels of the Mole guns and drape a blinding scarf around the observation posts in the lighthouse. Unit H (*C.M.B.s 5 and 7*) swung out in a wide circle which would take them into the bight of the Mole to carry out torpedo attacks on enemy destroyers moored alongside, and *C.M.B.s 21B* and *26B* swung the other way, to lob their Stokes bombs over the Mole parapet.

Gradually the already low visibility closed in. White metallic-tasting clouds of Brock smoke thickened and rose, and as each ship in turn nosed forward into the acrid fog, contact was lost between craft. Enveloping all, the clouds moved with them, renewed by the C.M.B.s, drifted in by the faintly perceptible northerly wind. Now every member of the fleet lived on borrowed time in a world of choking smoke and roaring engines, counting out the seconds until the enemy should react; but for a few more brief, expanding moments the night was theirs alone.

Then lazily—whitely—a star-shell burst to seaward, making daylight beyond the screen, and searchlights poked inquiring fingers up into the sky.

The German defenses awoke to danger. It was 11:50 P.M.

The smoke was close inshore now, masking everything. Aboard the C.M.B.s an impudent excitement held everyone as the swift craft danced forward and back, in and out of concealment of their own smoke screens, inviting attack. Under the Mole Extension guns, Welman heard shouts as the German gun-crews sought information and instructions. Sporadic small-arms fire spattered the water and a machine gun coughed in short, uncertain bursts: but still, while the enemy groped and pondered, the battle remained unjoined.

Then, with a baying roar which split open the last silence of the night, shore batteries fired blind, and heavy shells screamed overhead to plunge harmlessly into the sea far beyond the last units of the approaching fleet.

Relief washed through the blood: at last there could be no more turning back.

At 11:56—the most crucial moment of the approach —as though it grudged the help it had given and now sought satanically to undo it, the wind changed. During a few incredible seconds the night which had been black and dense turned greyly opaque, then crystal clear as the smoke moved solidly north. Metal tore up the surface of the water around the revealed C.M.B.s, the M.L.s, and the plunging destroyers as they circled back, smoke pouring from stacks, exhausts and canisters in an attempt to repair the gaps torn by the treacherous wind.

Then, less than a quarter of a mile from the Mole end, shouldering aside the remnants of the fog like a bull-terrier coming out of long grass, the *Vindictive* suddenly appeared. She seemed to pause for a split second just clear of the receding cloud and blackly silhouetted against its now silvered screen; then on she came, gathering speed and weight for the attack.

But however fast she moved, she had at least four minutes in the open sights of the Mole Extension guns. There were six of these—four 105-mm. and two 88-mm. —and at that range they could hardly miss. To those who watched it seemed that the whole operation was doomed. *Vindictive* could never reach the Mole.

# 6

FOR CARPENTER—until the moment when *Vindictive* had
burst from the smoke screen—the night had been one of
continuous but expected strain and responsibility, coupled with a curious lack of excitement. Even when his
ship entered the Brock smoke and visibility was cut to a
few feet so that he could not see even the forecastle,
there was no sudden jab of anxiety—certainly nothing of
panic. Rosoman's voice came regularly and imperturbably every minute through the voice pipe from the conning-tower under the bridge, with the arranged routine
question—"Are you all right, sir?"—and in the *Flammenwerfer* hut at the port end of the forebridge which gave
such an excellent view of the ship from bow nearly to
stern, Carpenter could take due satisfaction from the
smooth precision with which they had proceeded so far
and which now would surely take them to a perfect land-
fall on the Mole.

There had been no shattering explosions to tell of shallow undiscovered mines or forewarn the enemy; no ominous shuddering of keelson over unknown and treacherous shoal. Perfect planning had been rewarded: faith had
been justified.

Then in a second the whole position changed.

From being a potent hidden aggressor, *Vindictive* was
stripped of her cloak and advantage by the wind, and reduced to a looming target beneath heavy guns. In
the moment of revelation two thoughts exploded together
in Carpenter's brain: first, their position, course and
speed were exactly right, and second, unless he altered all
three very quickly his ship would be reduced to a drifting
hulk in a matter of minutes.

Years of training as a professional officer in a proud
Navy told: with the promptness of a reflex action and the
exactitude of a modern calculating machine he gave or-

ders to conning-tower and engine-room which would close ship to Mole at a different angle and at full speed; then as *Vindictive* swung to starboard and the whole length of the Mole extension came into view, he waited, poised and watchful, for the inevitable. Deliberately the British guns remained silent until discovery was certain: his ship vibrated under him with the increased power.

There was a void in time while all aboard held their breath, then six yellow-white flowers bloomed at regular intervals along the Mole extension and the night was filled with screaming metal as every gun in *Vindictive*'s foretop and port battery replied. Infernal clangor stunned the senses—but the ship held course.

Shell after shell hurtled across the rapidly-narrowing gap between the ship and the Mole, and as she swung in on her new course, she presented to the German gunners a target which grew in size until it was half the length of the extension from which they fired, and nearly twice the height—it was literally true that they could not miss her. *Vindictive* was perhaps two hundred yards from the easternmost gun when fire was opened on her and by the time she was abreast of number 6 at the western end, the range was down to fifty yards: heavy shell thudded into her, machine gun and rifle bullets streamed over like a driven cloud.

But still she steamed doggedly on, flames now shooting from her torn funnels, sparks and glowing steel fragments cascading from her upper works.

Two shells entered the forecastle and put the forward howitzer out of action, killing the crew—then another killed the relief crew from the port battery; two more tore through the hull just below the bridge, the first exploding on impact, the second entering and wrecking everything in the vicinity. The upper and false decks were furrowed and in parts plowed up, the bridge protection ripped to shreds, several of the all-important gangways reduced to matchwood, some of the Stokes- and Lewis-gun crews shot down and the remainder showered with white-hot shrapnel—but the ship steamed on.

To Carpenter and the other occupant of the *Flammenwerfer* hut—Lieutenant Eastlake, R.E., in charge of the flame-thrower—the spectacle was coldly enthralling; to the men in the foretop crouched over the chattering Lewis-guns and pom-poms and to the sweating gun-crews, it was flame and anger; to the men waiting below it was ice in their bowels.

Blood stained the decks as men dragged and carried the wounded down to the waiting surgeon: already he was too busy.

*Vindictive* was rolling now in the recoil from her own guns, in the impact from the enemy, in the swift flow and surge of her growing speed through shoal waters. Still her own guns fired; still shell tore through her stacks and whining fragments found living targets. Still she steamed on.

And now she had closed almost to safety—for this was the secret with which Carpenter had defeated the Mole artillerymen: this and their own lack of cool thought. The Germans were so sure that *Vindictive* was in their power that they had fired without pattern or plan, rightly certain that they could not miss. Every shell, every bullet, every bomb had hit her, but the targets had not been selective: men had died—but not the ship. Neither boilers nor steering gear were damaged during the first crucial hundred yards of closing spurt—and after that, every yard gained took them closer under the parapet until *Vindictive*'s vitals were protected by the Mole itself. Her upper works were in ribbons, but she was still sea-worthy—and now she was reaching the area where the Mole guns tended to mask each other.

She bumped against the Mole one minute late—at 0001 on St. George's Day: Mrs. Keyes had been right.

But if *Vindictive* was only one minute late, she was sadly out of position. She was also rolling from side to side like a dinghy in a liner's wash, and every roll did further damage to the essential landing-brows. Her speed through shallowing water had built up an enormous surge, now trapped between her side and the concrete Mole, and thrashing to burst free. Up and down the waters leaped, forced up by the following undercurrent, dropping back into the void left as the surge bounced away from the base of the Mole; boiling up and spewing out again as *Vindictive* bucked and reared in the turmoil.

In an endeavor to edge back towards the correct position—for their speed had taken them far past the fortified zone at the Mole end—Carpenter rang engines astern. The huge screws churned, *Vindictive* rocked sideways like a baby's cradle, and anchor derricks and gangways ground themselves to pieces on the parapet. Carpenter could see over the top now, and identified a long, low shadow as number 3 shed. They were nearly a quarter of a mile too far westward, but time was pressing and the landing parties must go ashore. He ordered the starboard anchor to be let go and held the ship steady by alternately reversing engines until it grappled. By now the din had risen in a crescendo and he could not be certain that his orders had reached the cable-party through the voice-pipe. He had heard no reply from them and the ship still hung loose in the maelstrom. He ordered Rosoman below to investigate. Eastlake in the hut with him gave orders to switch on the flamethrower but just at that moment a piece of shrapnel neatly sliced off the nozzle: the lives of everyone in the immediate vicinity were only saved by the fact that the pipes bringing up fuel for the dreadful weapon had already been cut by shellfire.

Then news came from the cable-deck. The starboard anchor had been let go but was unaccountably jammed and nothing could budge it. Carpenter ordered the port anchor to be dropped at the foot of the wall, and rang the engines astern again until a hundred yards of cable had been veered out. When the cable was snubbed, *Vindictive* brought up sharp and swung away from the Mole. With helm to starboard she went in again, but her bows were now so tight to the Mole that her stern jutted clear and the remaining gangways failed to reach the parapet-top. Helm amidships put the ship parallel but with the gap so wide that the brows wouldn't reach at all—and with the helm to port she swung far out again. Every enemy gun within two miles had now found *Vindictive* and was endeavoring to hit her. Above the level of the parapet-top she was like a sieve, and from the hellish din she might have been trapped in the heart of a gigantic thunderstorm.

Then *Iris* chugged sedately along her starboard flank, and *Daffodil* arrived. The tow had parted nearly an hour previously and only by cutting a corner and flogging engines to bursting-point had they arrived now. An unlucky shot had hit *Daffodil*'s bridge and her captain was wounded in the head and half blind. Nevertheless, he put her blunt nose expertly against *Vindictive*'s starboard beam, and pinned her bodily to the Mole so that at last the two remaining serviceable gangways could be dropped on to the parapet. The landing parties came out from below *Vindictive*'s false deck and stormed across them.

These assault parties were now all led by junior officers—for one simple and tragic reason. The men who had organized and trained them were dead, shot down as they stood waiting in too-exposed positions for the moment of attack. Colonel Elliot and his second-in-command, Major Cordner, had been on the bridge when the first salvo from the Mole guns had screamed across and they were both killed instantly. Captain Halahan who commanded the Bluejackets died on the false deck just below them, and Commander Edwards beside him was shot through both legs: when he ordered two of his men to carry him up the gangway on to the Mole, they took him below instead with understandable disobedience and thereby saved his life. Lieutenant-Commander A. L. Harrison, who was next in direct command, was unconscious with a smashed jaw and Hilton Young's right hand had been shattered by a passing shell; Lieutenant Walker had lost an arm. Chamberlain in command of 'B' Bluejacket Company was dead.

One detachment commander alone remained—Lieutenant-Commander Bryan Adams—and he was the first man on the Mole, leading his Bluejackets of 'A' Company across a shuddering, heaving plank which rose and fell several feet at one end with the rocking of the ship, while the outboard end sawed back and forth across the parapet and frequently came near to sliding off and precipitating everyone thirty feet down towards certain death. The first arrivals set about securing the Mole anchors of the assault craft. Incredibly, despite the hail of fire which swept flatly over their heads, the Mole appeared deserted.

A hundred yards further west, the officers leading 'D' Bluejacket Company and 'A' Company of the Royal Marines were facing similar troubles. *Iris*, too, was rocking through nightmare angles; in addition the scaling ladders were too short. Lieutenant Claude Hawkins, R.N., balanced himself on the top of one of them—held upright by his men—grabbed the parapet-top as he swayed towards it, pulled himself up and scrambled astride until he could turn and secure the ladder. Enemy soldiers immediately attacked him and he was last seen defending himself with his revolver. In an endeavor to succeed where Hawkins had failed, Lieutenant-Commander G. N. Bradford climbed the port anchor derrick, judged his moment perfectly and jumped the gap, carrying the grappling-anchor with him. As he hooked it into position a stream of machine-gun bullets lifted him off the parapet-top and dropped him between *Iris* and the Mole —and with the deep loyalty of the Service, Petty Officer Hallihan gave his life trying to recover his body.

Bradford's act was to earn for his family the second posthumous Victoria Cross in just over eighteen months: his brother had won the cross in command of a battalion of the Durhams at Eaucort l'Abbaye on October 1, 1916.

To the east, the Mole defenders were loath to approach *Vindictive* too closely. The fighting foretop was above the parapet and, despite the fact that it was now the principal target for enemy hostility, was still pouring out an accurate fire at every sign of life on the Mole itself and on the German destroyers which could now be seen moored on the inner side. The foretop was commanded by Lieutenant C. Rigby, R.M.A., Commander Osborne having turned it over to him when he went below to supervise the laying and firing of the remaining howitzers.

Rigby's instructions were to cover the landing party. He and his men engaged every enemy gun within range, switching targets continually, pinning the Germans down and destroying strongpoints: it was undoubtedly due to their efforts that for the first few minutes Adams and his men of 'A' Company were virtually undisturbed. Then two heavy shells crashed in and the foretop was reduced in a second to a tangled nest of smoking guns, exploding ammunition and blood-soaked, writhing bodies. From this chaos, one grimfaced, blackened, lantern-jawed figure clawed his way back to the rail, found a workable Lewis-gun, mounted it and took up the fight again: enemy machine gunners grown too presumptuous in the brief pause leaped back for cover and died if their reflexes were slow. Serjeant Norman Augustus Finch was demonstrating an essential indestructibility—even when another heavy shell blew his gun back off the rail on top of him and completed the wreck of the foretop, he retained sufficient hold on life and strength to find and carry the only other still-breathing occupant down tattered ladders and along crowded mess-decks to the sick bay. There he collapsed from his own wounds, but some weeks later he was able to receive the second V.C. won that night, standing erect by his hospital bed.

Meanwhile Wing-Commander Brock had decided that the time had come for him to collect his reward for the months of unremitting work and brilliant inventiveness. He had been somewhat disappointed that *Vindictive* had brought up so far from the Mole guns, for he had thus been unable to prove his assertion that his flamethrowers would deal with the German gunners unaided. Even more disappointing was the fact that when at last he had tried to switch on, all that happened was that thick and extremely inflammable oil flooded over the decks due to shrapnel smashing the ignition apparatus at the crucial moment. But that was now in the past: he had dealt effectively with the results and it was time for him to put a few of his other ideas into operation. There were some new phosphorus grenades he particularly wanted to see in action and there was also that matter of the sound-ranging apparatus on the Mole to investigate.

Handing over command of the pyrotechnics on board *Vindictive* to his chief assistant Graham Hewlett, and accompanied by one of his air-mechanics, Brock ran quickly over the plunging gangway and joined Adams on the Mole.

By now attempts to fix the grappling-irons had been abandoned. Despite several men sitting on top of the parapet (just the place in a night attack), despite also Rosoman's attempt to emulate Bradford's feat by climbing up the derrick, the grappling-anchors had proved too heavy to maneuver by hand, and eventually the foremost hoisting davit had been smashed against the Mole by one of *Vindictive*'s wilder lurches, and the steel prongs crashed down into the sea.

However, no further time could be spared, for the allocated duty for Adams and his men was to destroy the Mole Extension guns before the blockships arrived. It had been planned that they should be landed right on top of them, but they now had to make a 250-yard advance before they even reached their objective. The survivors of Adams's own company (half of them had become casualties on *Vindictive*) and some men of 'B' Company had now reached the Mole, and he led them swiftly eastward towards the guns. Forty yards past the stern of *Vindictive* they found a concrete observation post with what appeared to be a range-finding system rigged above it, and with the intense satisfaction of a man pursuing his hobby despite all minor distractions, Brock went forward to investigate. He allowed himself to be restrained long enough for a hand-grenade to be tossed in, then vanished through the entrance producing spanners and wrenches from his pockets with something of the air of an aggressive conjurer.

There was an iron ladder abreast of the concrete post and Adams sent some men down it to deal with enemy soldiers who were trying to escape from quarters below to the dubious security of the destroyers moored on the far side of the Mole. Some men he prudently left to guard the top of the ladder, then led the remainder in a rush further along the road towards the Mole guns: they were now reaching the fortified zone at the end of the Mole proper, which it had been intended to attack from inside.

He and his party were subject to heavy fire. In addition to the illumination supplied by explosions, star-shell and flares, one of the pyrotechnic party was firing off rockets through *Vindictive*'s stern portholes in order to silhouette the lighthouse for the approaching blockships. These burst brilliantly above the Mole—and the Bluejacket assault party advancing along the parapet roadway were as easy to spot as the targets in a well lighted shooting-gallery.

From behind constructed stone trenches machine-gun fire swept the roadway, a small party of the enemy who had been courageously advancing to meet them fired a concerted and well placed volley before retreating rapidly, and the machine guns and pom-poms of the enemy destroyers were now released for wider action by the elimination of Serjeant Finch from the contest. Adams's party dwindled sadly. At last the few gallant survivors went to ground and Adams himself returned to find reinforcements.

He found three new arrivals at the concrete post— Petty Officer Antell and two Lewis-gunners. Antell was in considerable pain due to multiple wounds of hand and arm and was firmly ordered back aboard the *Vindictive*. The two Lewis-gunners went forward, and in their advance were joined and then led by the huge, slightly-swaying figure of Lieutenant-Commander Harrison who had recovered consciousness aboard *Vindictive,* hurled himself across the gangway before anyone could stop him, and despite the physical torture and mental perplexity caused by a badly-fractured jaw and concussion, now arrived to take firm control. He listened to Adams's report, ordered him back to request Royal Marine reinforcements, then went forward and joined the remnants of the Bluejacket assault force.

He had successfully led too many assaults to allow his men to be trapped into a static position, and he had his party on their feet and racing forward again in a matter of seconds. Harrison had spirit and a good sense of tactics; unfortunately he lacked hitting-power and light automatic support fire. True, Able Seaman McKenzie was at his side, but a Lewis-gun is unhandy and its weight with sufficient ammunition to be really effective is crippling. Inevitably the rush lost momentum as withering fire cut down the numbers. They were on a brilliantly lit stage, and far enough from their objective for riflemen to take

Rear-Admiral Sir Rosslyn Wemyss.

Admiral Lord Keyes: from portrait by de Laszlo.

H.M.S. *Vindictive* shortly after commissioning.

Gangways over which the assault parties landed from *Vindictive*.

Close-up of the canal mouth at low tide. Scar in sandbank shows where *Intrepid* first grounded.

View of the canal mouth looking seaward, showing blockships after the battle.

H.M.S. *Brilliant* and *Sirius* aground off Ostend.

H.M.S. *Vindictive* at Dover after the Zeebrugge raid.

Aerial view of Zeebrugge canal mouth at high tide, showing
blockships in position.

Close-up of *Iphigenia,* with *Intrepid* in background.

This view of one of *Vindictive's* funnels gives an idea of the gunfire she faced.

The remains of the viaduct, after *C3* exploded under it.

Lt. G. N. Bradford, R.N.

Lt. R. D. Sandford, R.N.

AWARDED THE
VICTORIA CROSS

Serjeant Finch, R.M.L.I.

Able Seaman MacKenzie

Lt. V. A. C. Crutchley, R.N.

Capt. E. Banford, R.M.L.I.

AWARDED

THE

VICTORIA

CROSS

Lt.-Cdr. R. Bourke, R.N.V.R.

Lt. P. T. Dean, R.N.V.R.

Lt.-Cdr. G. H. Drummond, R.N.V.R.

deliberate aim. At last Harrison fell, and McKenzie and Able Seaman Eaves went to ground—both badly-wounded but still determined.

McKenzie got his sights on the trench positions and swept up and down them until running figures burst from cover, then he shot them down as they ran. Eaves managed to hoist Harrison's body across his shoulders and tried to run back with him, but was repeatedly hit himself until he too fell, some way from the look-out post. He was eventually taken prisoner.

McKenzie managed to crawl back—still lugging his Lewis-gun, despite his wounds.

In the meantime, westward and abreast of the *Vindictive*, the Marines were in action. Their original tasks had been to drop down on top of the fortified zone at the far end of the Mole proper and from there cover the Bluejackets wrecking the Mole guns, then to advance westward out through the fortifications and down the Mole as protection for the demolition parties blowing up the sheds, cranes and all other dock installations within reach. Once more the position of the *Vindictive* complicated the tasks and a desperate shortage of manpower made matters worse. Nearly seven hundred officers and men of the R.M.L.I. had sailed with the convoy; of these the whole of 'A' company were virtually marooned in the *Iris*, and of the main body who had travelled in *Vindictive* far too many had died on the decks or been shot down as they debouched on to the Mole. Incredibly, during the entire debarkation, no one had been killed crossing the gangways, either by enemy fire or the far greater danger of toppling off the see-sawing planks and falling between ship and Mole.

Colonel Elliot and Major Cordner were dead, and command now devolved upon Major Weller, commanding 'C' Company from Plymouth. He decided that he must first secure the landward approaches to ensure that the essential line of communication and retreat to *Vindictive* remained open.

He sent Lieutenant T. F. V. Cooke with the men of number 5 platoon westwards along the parapet roadway, where they eventually reached a position some two hundred yards in front of *Vindictive*. They had silenced a party of snipers who had been only too effective from the end of number 2 shed, and now they provided covering fire for men of 9 and 10 platoons who had lowered themselves by ropes down on to the Mole proper. Under the leadership of Lieutenant C. D. R. Lamplough, these latter crossed the Mole in a storming rush, formed a strongpoint at the western end of number 3 shed which commanded the land approaches, thus securing the first objective and establishing a firm base for a possible assault on one of the enemy destroyers.

Now number 7 platoon under Lieutenant H. A. P. de Berry descended scaling ladders placed in position by Sergeant-Major Thatcher, joined Lamplough's men, and under over-all command of Captain Bamford began to form up for the second objective—an attack on the fortified position at the Mole end. By now Cooke's advance party had become the focus of enemy machine guns further on down the Mole and like the Bluejacket party to the east, were suffering dreadfully from the lack of cover. Cooke himself was hit twice and eventually lost consciousness, and Private Press, himself wounded, carried him back to the ship. With Lamplough's party now in position, there was no further necessity for this advance post. The survivors of number 5 platoon carried their wounded back to safety and those fit enough to do so dropped down to join the assembling forces under Bamford.

Then Adams arrived at the gangways with the request from Harrison that Weller send reinforcements east along the parapet wall. He sent Lieutenant Underhill with men of numbers 11 and 12 platoons, but time was passing too quickly and the blockships were drawing closer and closer to the still all-powerful Mole batteries. The din, the smoke, the confusion rose to a crescendo and gradually the initiative passed to the defenders as the element of surprise dissipated and the German gunners brought more and more of their emplaced guns into action. Ashore, military commanders had by now made up their minds as to the pattern of the attack, and were issuing their orders. Grey-clad figures raced through the narrow Zeebrugge streets buckling on their equipment.

In addition to the inferno actually raging on the Mole and around the assault craft, the 15-inch shells of the monitors *Erebus* and *Terror* were landing with thunderous regularity only a mile or so away, and shore batteries were replying. To this uproar *Vindictive*'s 11-inch howitzer was adding its not inconsiderable quota, and her 6-inch guns were reaching a stage of near-incandescence. It is thus somewhat doubtful if the urgent requests for reinforcements yelled down the lighthouse telephone by the frantic German guard commander, or his sudden, startled announcement of the appearance of the blockships, were either heard or understood by his superior in shore barracks.

However, the Mole gunners had also seen the blockships, and the Extension guns were swinging around to command the inner approaches and blow these new arrivals out of the water. As further reinforcement, a half-battalion of German infantry were converging on the shore end of the Mole, and its leading company—on bicycles—were already pedalling furiously along the causeway.

On the Mole, the Marines and Bluejackets of the assault force were now hemmed in on three sides: they could not burrow for protection into the solid concrete and it was becoming increasingly dangerous to raise one's head sufficiently to peer along the weapon sights. They clung to the wet shadows and fought bitterly.

The sides of the trap closed in.

# 7

ACCORDING TO the prepared timetable, the three vessels of Unit K—the two submarines and their attendant picket-boat—should have slipped their tows 56 minutes after passing 'G' buoy and after a brief pause for taking up station, shaped their own course for the viaduct.

When the time came, however, *C 3*—having followed the instructions thus far to the letter—found that her two consorts were no longer in company. Once her own towing hawser had been cleared from the destroyer *Trident* and that vessel had disappeared into the night, *C 3* found herself vastly alone on a gently heaving sea. This condition would be no matter for concern for submariners in normal circumstances but with the particular task which now lay ahead of *C 3* the absence of her sister-ship was disturbing and that of the picket-boat critical.

Not that these gaps in establishment had much effect upon the younger Sandford. Possessed of an irrepresible optimism since birth, his gleeful spirit was quite capable of interpreting the situation as nothing more serious than a race to the viaduct, with the first explosion as the winner —and by a piece of unwarranted good luck, he had a head start. His brother in the picket-boat had been absent as far back as 'G' buoy (the picket-boat had in fact very nearly capsized owing to a difficult following sea, and only the timely parting of the tow had saved it), so *C 3* could count on at least ten minutes start over her. As for *C 1*— her tow must have parted since then, but as the surrounding seas were empty as far as could be seen, *C 3* must be at least a mile in front.

With a quick glance at his watch to check timing (it was now 11:39 P.M.) Dick Sandford ordered the necessary adjustment of course, and travelling for the time being on her petrol engines, *C 3* slid gently through the water at a pleasant eight and a half knots. Below, the atmosphere was cool and fresh—for a submarine. The motors throbbed encouragingly, and after the lurching and jarring they had suffered during the tow (the power steering had been fractured as a result of this) the steady forward motion gave a cheerful sense of purpose.

Their captain's high spirits always infected the crew—all just as young as he in heart, if not quite in years—and at the wheel his First Lieutenant, John Howell-Price, felt an expanding urge to sing. Petty Officer Harner, on the other hand, silently watched the gauges and cast an experienced eye over the twelve charges of Amatol packed in the bows. The immediate present was as far as he would allow his thoughts to wander: of all on board, Harner was probably the one who realized most clearly the hazards which lay before them.

On the conning-tower, life was cool, lightly damp, exhilarating: the sea hissed along the smooth steel bulges ten feet below. Sandford wondered what his father, the Archdeacon, was doing at the moment and concluded that he was most probably fast asleep in bed: then his thoughts passed to the possible activities of his six elder brothers in general, and to those of Francis in particular. Thoughts of Francis brought him back to present realities. He kept at bay presentiments of what might happen if Francis failed to turn up at all by picturing the effects of the proposed explosion of *C 3* under the viaduct: it really was fantastic luck, this opportunity to set off what would undoubtedly be the most gigantic bang of a lifetime.

Meantime, with ingrained precision, he automatically kept check of time and course, and his ear registered the soft regular beat of the outdated but still reliable engines. It was nearly time to switch over to the batteries: he had no intention of submerging even partly if it could be avoided, for the tide was lower than had been originally reckoned and he wanted to ram his guided bomb as high up under the floor of the viaduct as he could get it. But if they were attacked by surface craft, he would have to dive. As he passed the order to cut the petrol engines and bring in the motors, a deep rumble started away to port, and white light burst high in the eastern sky.

It was suddenly quiet in the submarine. Someone came

silently to the foot of the steel ladder and stood there for a moment, but nothing was said and the listener moved away; the night had turned cold, and the steel rail was like ice in his hands.

*C 3* was still alone on a gently heaving sea.

Just before midnight they came to a drifting smoke screen and for a few seconds were blind in its unfamiliar, dry pungency; but it was moving northwards quickly now and they were soon clear of it. To the northeast, the night suddenly burst open in shell-blast where *Vindictive* was steaming into history.

At midnight, they were one and a half miles from the viaduct, and with a silent tribute to his brother's planning and accuracy Dick ordered a change of course to approach the steel bridge at right angle to its length. There was the devil's own thunder going on two miles to port, and he could picture the gunners firing like shelling peas. No one had spotted *C 3* as yet—but how long would that last?

With a crack of astonishing violence a star-shell burst immediately overhead, then shore batteries opened fire. Fifty yards to port grey geysers mushroomed from the sea. *C 3* rolled, but kept course. Two more geysers erupted and the shell-scream followed overhead—then surprisingly, the firing ceased. Leading Seaman Cleaver turned on the smoke canisters, but the wind drifted the clouds offshore and slightly ahead, so it failed to hide them, screening the viaduct instead. Cleaver turned the smoke off again and came back aft to the bridge.

On they ran, knowing they were watched, waiting for the shellfire mysteriously withheld. Then a flare burst somewhere just above the water inside the sweep of the Mole, and the whole viaduct was blackly silhouetted against its yellow glow. The piers rose slim but solid, the braces were a web between them, the palisade a wide black margin above. There was movement in the gaps in the bottom quarter of the margin, and an unrecognizable fuzziness among the piers just below it. Then the flare died.

*C 3* ran on towards a viaduct which was beginning to loom up.

Two searchlights stabbed down upon them, one from each end of the viaduct, then a third joined in from somewhere ashore near the root of the causeway. On the conning tower, the hard, white light baked the remaining moisture from tongues and mouths gone dry, and salt crystallized on lips and in the furrows above the eyes.

And still the enemy held their fire.

Sandford made the last alteration of course exactly 100 yards from the viaduct. The piers could be seen clearly and the caverns between, with the waiting foe above. As the submarine swung slightly to port, aiming precisely between two of the piers, a thought flickered for a second at the back of Sandford's mind—but was gone before he could catch it.

The sands were running out now and the men must not be trapped below. Sandford ordered them up and they stood crowded together on the bridge, staring ahead as the steel trap loomed higher before them. The gap narrowed. Fascinated, they watched and forgot to breathe.

Then *C 3* swept on into black shadow beneath the steel platform, rocked up for'ard like a bucking horse, and with the rasping clangor of ten million files on sheet steel flung herself over and on to the bridgework of girders at nine and a half knots. She only stopped when her conning-tower smashed against solid steel above. All around her cross-braces snapped and molten globules from the scarified hull hissed in the water below. She had ridden up two feet: the floor of the viaduct was less than twelve feet above the steel casing of her bows, which jutted just beyond the far side of the viaduct into the Mole harbor.

Five tons of Amatol rested centrally under the floor of the viaduct.

And still—for the moment—the only signs of life from the enemy close around were the sounds of shouting, of boots on steel plates and of laughter. The Germans were under the impression that the *C 3*—apparently ignorant of the narrow spaces between the viaduct piers—had been attempting to run under the viaduct and into the Mole harbor. Now, they believed, they had caught a British submarine, possibly slightly damaged but basically intact.

And having caught the submarine, they had no intention of allowing the crew to escape.

While Sandford remained on the conning tower to fire the fuse, the others scrambled fore and aft to release the motor-skiff hanging from spars lashed horizontally across the tower. There had been two of these, one each side, but the port one had gone—where and how? The lashings were slipped, the skiff dropped away and as the ropes ran out it bumped down on to *C 3*'s bulges and slid outwards into the water. As the crew piled aboard, there was a sharp and ominous clank, but in the flurry no one noticed.

Then Sandford ripped clean the end of the cordtex, struck it—setting off the long, twelve-minute time fuse—came down off the conning tower like a sack of coals into the skiff. With a lurch the tiny craft yawed clear of the *C 3* and wallowed deep-loaded out from the shadows into the open. Immediately there were screams of anger and barked orders, drowned by the hard stammer of machine guns and the louder, vicious crack of rifles. Flame stabbed down upon the skiff from less than twenty feet above and splinters whipped up from the flimsy hull. The searchlights burst alight again, their beams pinning the skiff down on the sea for the defenders to riddle with fire; lead shrilled close between the tight-packed men and smacked through wood, and the sea jetted inboard through a dozen holes.

Stoker Henry Cullis Bindall bit back a grunt and grabbed at the gunwale, and as Sandford's hand went out to help him it seemed to explode in blood. The water slopping in the bottom of the skiff stained bright red, but it lessened in volume as the specially installed pump sprang to life and vomited it over the side again.

The skiff-motor, although operating, whirred uselessly: as the skiff had hit the water, the propeller had smacked hard against the *C 3*'s exhaust and the shaft had snapped. Allan Roxburgh and Petty Officer Harner each manned one of the skiff's diminutive oars but Harner was hit, gasped and rolled sideways off the thwart. The skiff was still only a few yards from the *C 3*, with a westward set of tide trying to sweep her back under the viaduct, three men out of six were already wounded, and the fire concentrated on them was as thick as raindrops in a summer shower.

As Leading Seaman Cleaver flung himself down in Harner's place, Dick Sandford was hit again and more seriously. He just controlled a convulsive leap which might have capsized the rolling skiff, then gripped his thigh in order to staunch the spurting blood. His face was already white from the tearing agony of a hand wound and the faces of the others blanched at the red torrent which first drenched and then matted his trouser-leg. He rolled away from the tiller and John Howell-Price took command.

Gradually Cleaver and Roxburgh pulled the wallowing, stricken craft out into the waters clear of the Mole; the tide pressed inexorably against them, the oars were trifling, pom-poms from the shore added heavier metal to the leaden hail and inboard the prospect was heartbreaking. Dick Sandford could grin weakly at them to cheer them on, but Bindall was speechless and Harner near unconscious in the bows where he had dragged himself out of the way.

John Howell-Price kept them going. He came out of his habitual reserve as though he wore it only as part of the uniform of a first lieutenant, and suddenly revealed a personality as clear and strong as Sandford's own—and Dick, who had picked him from a hundred friends who had pestered him for the position, could concentrate upon quelling the demands of his own imperious pain. As the blood clotted and staunched, and the dreadful agony in his hand ebbed before the numbing of the nerves, he remembered something: that faint, elusive thought which had flickered at the back of his mind at the moment of the last turn into the viaduct, came back to him.

It had been a plaintive reminder by a long-ignored instinct of self-preservation that if he had any intention of using the gyro-control gear, that was the moment to abandon ship and send the *C 3* in unmanned.

John Howell-Price glanced quickly down at his captain. A sense of humor was all very well, but this was no time to start laughing—even for Dick. Had his wounds affected his brain?

Before he had time to investigate, however, *C 3* blew up.

The skiff was abreast of the end of the viaduct now, having been pulled northwestwards by the tide: *C 3* lay not more than two hundred yards from her—probably much less—and yet such was the enveloping thunder of the battle that the explosion was more seen than heard.

As Roxburgh and Cleaver prayed for more strength and Dick Sandford fought off another wave of pain; as, a mile to the east, de Berry and Lamplough with their Marines fought to hold their bitterly contested footholds, and further east still, Harrison charged forward to his gallant end, a sudden yellow-white light flooded and consolidated the stark details of the scene. From the viaduct a pillar of flame mounted higher and higher into the air and as it rose, the dark outlines of flying girders, railway sleepers, guns and twisted bodies were silhouetted against its brilliance.

Leading Seaman Potter, from his vantage point in the conning tower of *Iphigenia* as she swung in past the lighthouse and shaped course for the canal entrance, noticed other, vaguely unbelievable shapes. Narrow-rimmed wheels spun out across the water, familiarly-bent metal tubes and frames showed momentarily against the white screen: then, perfect and unmistakable, a complete bicycle, its rider still gripping the handlebars in a catalepsy of fright and astonishment, rode high into the air, somersaulted completely, and crashed down into the sea.

The rear files of the bicycle company, unable to stop in time, shot over the edge of the hole which had so unexpectedly opened in front of them and met their deaths in the sea or among the tangled web of steel girders; but theirs were the only bodies ever found, for the majority of the company was blown to pieces. The reinforcements would not now arrive: the pressure on the Marine and Bluejacket assault parties—if not relieved—could not be increased. Communication with the shore was cut.

In the tiny motor-skiff, relief and joy drained the remaining strength from nerves and muscles already overburdened. Not that it mattered—the searchlights had gone out and the fire bearing on them was lighter: the gunners behind the shore pom-poms were too much shaken by what they had just witnessed to maintain their fire on a target which was anyway no longer illuminated for them.

Ten minutes after the explosion, the picket-boat came down along the length of the Mole and a very worried and anxious Francis Sandford saw his brother and the crew of *C 3* brought inboard. As the picket-boat was crewed partly by other members of the original *C 3* complement, they could not have been in more considerate hands—but medical attention on board a picket-boat is limited, and Dick Sandford insisted that Bindall and Harner were given aid and made comfortable before he would allow even his brother to attend to his own wounds.

The story of the picket-boat and her crew that night is one first of near disaster and then of extreme anxiety. She was towed by the destroyer *Moorsom* but due to a following sea and an unexpected heaviness in handling, was twice on her beam ends. Francis Sandford's report adds, "It is by no means clear why she righted herself."

They were still in tow at 'D' buoy, but shortly afterwards the tow was fouled and delay occurred. When cleared, *Moorsom* tried to catch up to regain her convoy position. With the resultant increase of speed the tow parted completely. There was no adequate means of repair and time was pressing. In the hope that twelve knots could be wrung from the engines, Sandford took the picket-boat on under her own steam. It was soon only too evident that they were dropping further and further behind the timetable and Sandford's feelings—and indeed those of all his crew—can be well imagined.

They steered for the Mole hoping to hit it near the viaduct, but with the kind of luck they were having that night they just made the lighthouse. They turned westward as soon as their position was established, apparently missed the explosion by minutes, skirted the cauldron of fire which contained *Vindictive,* and then found the bobbing, pitiable skiff three minutes later.

Of *C 1* there was still no sign.

# 8

WITH THE viaduct blown and the blockships well on their way in, Carpenter proceeded to tour *Vindictive*. Although he was as yet completely unscathed, bearing apparently a charmed life, his uniform and accouterments bore curious marks. The peak of his cap looked rather as though the mice had been at it and a large hole gaped at the lower left hand corner of his cap badge. It was balanced by another similar hole at the back of the cap, through which some of the lining protruded and there was also an unseamanlike ridge across the crown. His binocular case slung behind him was not likely to be used again either, for shrapnel had passed through its length and his searchlight and smoke goggles hung with shattered lenses from the straps. Later he was to discover that his watch had been reduced to a case with loose works—altogether he was no longer the glass of fashion of the Naval staff officer.

As he descended from the bridge, one of the first sights to meet his eyes was that of Lieutenant E. Hilton Young, R.N.V.R., in his trousers and shirtsleeves, hatless, his right arm bandaged and a large cigar jutting imperturbably from a widely grinning face. He was supervising the work of the 6-inch port battery and had little time to waste on social pleasantries, even with his captain.

"Got one in the arm!" he announced shortly, in reply to inquiries, and before solicitude could suggest his removal to safer spheres, added importantly, "Ah, well. Got to get on, y'know!"

Later Hilton Young decided he'd better check on the Mole position. He was seen standing at the head of one of the gangways, still in his shirtsleeves, still hatless, still blandly puffing at his cigar as he gently rose and fell with the see-sawing of the plank, gazing appreciatively at the scenes of bitter fighting around him.

Carpenter's progress bore similarities to Dante's experiences in the Inferno. An angry and continual clangor rang from the funnels as shot reduced them to ribbons and ricocheted viciously between the upper works; white-hot shrapnel rained down on the decks, occasionally supplemented by a grey, vicious hail as low-fired shells smashed off pieces of the concrete parapet before howling flatly away into the darkness. *Vindictive* replied. Her mortars threw their screaming bombs over the Mole with regular explosions, the deck Lewis-guns drummed and chattered unceasingly, the howitzers boomed and cracked, huge rockets still whistled alarmingly from the stern ports.

Below decks, if the noise was slightly less the sights and smells were stupefying. Over all, the sickly reek of ether pervaded with its sinister connotations, penetrating even the thick heaviness of exploding cordite and that basic naval odor of tar and corticene. Men lay everywhere—in dark corners if they were dying and could reach them, propped against bulkheads, packing the mess-decks; the walking-wounded helped and consoled the bad cases, the stretcher bearers hurried to and fro, the excess crew who had come for the trip paid their passage a thousand times over in willing service. The surgeons sweated and snipped, the sick-bay attendants swabbed and bandaged.

And everyone wanted news of the battle.

"Have we won, sir? What's happening? Where are the blockships?"—the questions came to Carpenter from all sides as he made his way along, cheerful, encouraging, assured.

"That'll fix 'em, sir, won't it?" whispered one youngster propped in a corner, a smile of contentment spreading over his face as Carpenter told of probable success. The boy's head fell back against the steel bulkhead but the smile remained. "Blast 'em . . ." he whispered as he died.

In the engine room harsh yellow light glinted through the blue and black jungle and the air was thick with grease and sweat and heat, and the faint sourness of men controlling fear with their minds while denied the blessed release of action. Engine-room and stokehold men know too much of death; they have time to think and everywhere they look they see the pipes of scalding steam, the boilers, the fires, the jetting oil; around them steel flails sob as they plunge and rise again.

To add to the closed, trapped atmosphere, ammonia fumes had leaked into the engine room and stokeholds shortly before the arrival at the Mole. During those last few minutes of the approach, while all hell raged outside and the crew expected to see gaping holes torn in the hull, they were forced to endure the extra heat and confinement of goggles and respirators. A few shell-splinters had fallen through but that was all; torpedo-netting piled on the gratings kept out the steel rain from the funnels. But the din had penetrated and told its own story; now they all crowded around Carpenter and found release for tense nerves in bursting cheers and hammerblows on shipmates' shoulders.

Carpenter returned to the bridge. There was little change in conditions—if anything, enemy fire on the upper works had increased. Pom-poms on one of the destroyers opposite were still proving a nuisance, although Lamplough and his Marines of 9 and 10 platoons had attacked the other with hand grenade and rifle, killing several of the crew and silencing the automatic fire.

Further eastward on the Mole, the main assault was going forward but the barbed-wire entanglements precluded a fast sweeping rush against emplaced automatic fire, and the foremost destroyer could still enfilade the flank of an attack. Small parties of Marines worked their way forward under the cover of rail trucks, and bitter, isolated fighting took place across the width of the concrete arena. Exploding shell filled the air with cordite fumes, and metal fragments pockmarked the stone, too often splattering crimson on the grey-white surface.

From the *Vindictive,* Carpenter watched the progress of the action. The blockships had gone past the lighthouse nearly half an hour before—at 0020—and by now they were undoubtedly resting on the sea-bed somewhere—it was to be hoped in the right place. Whether they had been successful or not, their crews by now must, with sheer passage of time, be either lost or rescued; *Vindictive*'s job was surely done, for at no time had there been anything but the heaviest possible concentration of fire upon her, and the diversion she had caused could not have been greater.

The assault parties had been promised twenty minutes' notice of *Vindictive*'s withdrawal and as the last permitted time for leaving the Mole was 0120, the retirement signal must be given in ten minutes anyway. Was there anything to be gained by staying until the last possible moment? Without definite information regarding the blockships he could not be absolutely certain, but one fact was evident; *Vindictive* was held in position solely by *Daffodil*'s efforts and if anything happened to the ferry-boat, then *Vindictive* would swing away and the storming parties on the Mole, unable to return aboard, would be lost. *Daffodil*'s position was far more vulnerable than *Vindictive*'s for she was further out, and her vitals were not screened by the mass of the Mole. Moreover Carpenter was beginning to think that some of the damage his ship was suffering came from the heavy shore batteries around Blankenberghe—to which *Vindictive* was tangentially unscreened and *Daffodil* thus completely exposed.

The responsibility was Carpenter's and he had no wish to share it: after a brief talk with Rosoman to ensure he had overlooked no vital point, he ordered the retirement signal sounded. As all horns and sirens aboard *Vindictive* had long since been shot away, orders were passed to *Daffodil* to use her horn. There was a half-anxious, half-comic interval while the ferry-boat's pipe spluttered and gurgled, drenching the neighbourhood with rusty foam, black-clotted sludge and luke-warm bathwater, then a low moan became audible, gradually increasing in volume as it rose up the scale until it was emitting a workmanlike, earsplitting yowl. This was repeated several times and retirement began.

It was fraught with difficulty and danger. There seems to be a deep atavistic streak in the British nature which will not allow its warriors to leave their dead on the field: no matter what the price demanded in life and limb, they bring their dead home.

Zeebrugge provided several almost unbelievable examples of this. Of the entire convoy strength, numbering nearly seventeen hundred men, only 49 failed to return to Dover and of these the sea had claimed some and others were prisoners for the very reason that they had refused to leave dangerously and often fatally wounded comrades. This is possibly absurd and probably wasteful: but it has grandeur.

Covered by Lewis-guns on the parapet and the Marines of number 9 platoon holding a tiny perimeter, the sound men on the Mole crossed in spasmodic rushes to the scaling-ladders and ropes, and pulled themselves the 16 feet up to the top—with their backs to an angry enemy and the weight of a wounded or dead comrade across their shoulders: man's spirit is his strength, and in exaltation or compassion his strength is limitless.

In a steady stream the men came down the gangways, often to lay down their burdens and return again to the raging battle to bring in another of the wounded. Padre Peshall's score will never be known—like Harrison he had played football and combined immense physical strength with his devotion.

With the signs of retreat obvious to the enemy, German fire and fury redoubled—it is always easier to be brave against a retreating foe, and indeed, then he is most vulnerable: Carpenter knew that the most dangerous time lay ahead. Since his return to the bridge he had already twice avoided death himself by only millimeters —once when a shell set fire to a stack of boxes containing fused Stokes bombs, and once by direct shellfire. In the first instance, the chief quartermaster, Petty Officer Youlton, dealt with the danger by stentorian orders to everyone in the vicinity (regardless of rank) to remove themselves, while he himself smashed open the burning boxes on the deck and stamped on the contents until they were extinguished. When the fire broke out again later, the position resolved itself into simple factors —which would last longer, the fire or Youlton's boots? It was a near thing, but Youlton received his Conspicuous

Gallantry Medal in hospital for reasons other than burnt feet—he was too closely connected with Carpenter's second narrow escape.

Nearly fifteen minutes had passed since the retirement signal, and the stream of survivors from the Mole was thinning. Lieutenant-Commander Rosoman, Carpenter and Youlton were standing outside the conning tower on the alert for the first possible moment of safe withdrawal, when a shell exploded just behind them. Rosoman fell with shrapnel through both legs, Youlton's arm was shattered and Carpenter received a deep flesh-wound in the left shoulder: he was remarkably lucky.

A few minutes later, he received assurances that the last of the attack force had come aboard, but to make doubly certain he went to look for himself. How he avoided death at that moment can never be known; he stood on the foremost gangway, solitary and unmoving, and surveyed the deserted scene. No man moved on the wide expanse of the Mole, but from its edges destruction came at him from every angle—and missed. Satisfied, he returned to the bridge and issued his orders.

*Daffodil* reversed engines and allowed *Vindictive* to swing away from the Mole, and a tow was passed to her from the bigger ship's bows. As *Daffodil* tugged the tow came taut—and snapped almost immediately. But *Vindictive*'s head had started to swing. It was enough: the anchor cable was slipped and Carpenter rang his engines full ahead. Gathering way, the big ship moved along the Mole and as her helm was put over, the last trick in the bag was pulled. Even denser clouds of Brock smoke than had been used in the approach belched from stacks and canisters aboard *Vindictive* and the two ferryboats. As the Germans prepared for a last gigantic onslaught which would wipe out the force which had inflicted this humiliation upon them their quarry disappeared completely from view in a screen as impenetrable and as extensive as the Mole itself—and this time the wind remained constant, gently blowing the screen after the retreating ships and warmly protecting them.

The Brock smoke had given them just sufficient cover to get in: now it was undoubtedly saving them all on the way out—but its resourceful and accomplished creator was missing. For some months afterwards there were persistent stories that Brock had been seen leading a party of Marines in the attack on German gun-positions, that he had attacked the enemy with his bare fists when his revolver was empty, that he removed breeches from the guns himself and flung them into the sea, that he had been wounded and that two Marines had refused to leave him and had last been seen locked in fierce hand-to-hand combat with enemy soldiers above his recumbent form.

The truth has never been established—the last certainty was his disappearance into the observation post, intent on solving the mysteries of German sound-ranging methods. Possessed of a brilliant, questing brain, a charming and affectionate personality, Brock was lost at the height of his powers. The more one reads his notes, his letters, and the opinions of those who knew him best, the greater certainty arises on one point: had he known of his fate beforehand, he would still have gone gaily forward to meet it.

So *Vindictive* left the Mole where she had won more glory in an hour than most ships do in their lifetimes. The gangways crashed over the side as they slid from the parapet, for a moment the wreckage fouled the port propeller but it soon cleared, the mainmast-bumpkin hammered the concrete as it carried out its destined duty protecting the screws and, with clear visibility in front and the densest fog behind, the gallant old ship pelted away into the night. Flames streamed from her gaping stacks until she appeared to be on fire, but her boilers pushed her along at a spanking 15 knots: despite her wounds she had every reason to be satisfied with her night's work.

The same, unfortunately, could not be said for all the assault craft. *Daffodil*, of course, had rendered sterling service. Had it not been for the enormous head of pressure which her engineers kept in her boilers, undoubtedly the storming of the Mole could not have taken place—the blockships would have been sunk before they reached the lighthouse. This achievement was even more remarkable in view of the fact that the engine room was holed and two compartments flooded, but Acting Artificer-Engineer Sutton dealt with the situation with cool and deliberate efficiency—and then returned to the hour-long task of keeping the hands of the pressure gauges at a point considerably past the danger line.

Some of the demolition party aboard *Daffodil* managed to climb up over her bows on to *Vindictive* and eventually reach the Mole (some of the explosive charges had been placed in position but were not blown because of the proximity of our own men)—but in the main her value had been as pin to her parent craft. Campbell had shown superb seamanship and was later most deservedly decorated for his bravery—wounded and half-blind, he had refused to leave the bridge until there was no likelihood whatever of accident or misfortune.

But for poor *Iris* it had been a bitter and frustrating night which ended in dire tragedy.

Despite the self-sacrifice of both Hawkins and Bradford, she had been unable to secure herself to the Mole. For a few minutes after Bradford's death, the anchor he had placed remained in position—but *Iris* was being flung about to a much greater extent even than *Vindictive,* and eventually the cable was either torn or shot away. Suddenly Commander Gibbs found his vessel surging far out from the Mole and swinging like a pendulum at the end of her starboard main anchor-cable which, unlike her parent ship, she had successfully let go upon first arrival.

Gibbs decided that with his scaling ladders broken and enemy personnel directly overhead, there was little chance of landing his Marines over the parapet. With the object, therefore, of landing them across *Vindictive* Gibbs slipped his anchor cable and steamed in a wide circle around the stern of *Daffodil* to come in on *Vindictive*'s quarter. There was unavoidable delay in securing alongside, for the attention of all on board the larger ships was concentrated on the fighting on the Mole, but eventually help was forthcoming.

Hardly was the task completed, however, when on Carpenter's orders *Daffodil* sounded the retirement signal and *Iris* was instructed to cast off and make her way

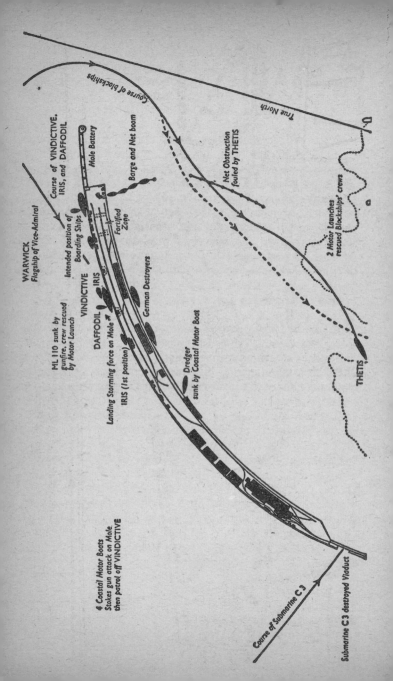

WARWICK
*Flagship of Vice-Admiral*

Course of VINDICTIVE, IRIS, and DAFFODIL

Mole Battery

Intended position of Boarding Ships

Barge and Net boom

Net Obstruction fouled by THETIS

Fortified Zone

2 Motor Launches rescued Blockships' crews

VINDICTIVE

IRIS

DAFFODIL

ML 110 sunk by gunfire, crew rescued by Motor Launch

German Destroyers

Landing Storming force on Mole

IRIS (1st position)

Dredger sunk by Coastal Motor Boat

THETIS

4 Coastal Motor Boats Stokes gun attack on Mole then patrol off VINDICTIVE

Course of Submarine C 3

Submarine C 3 destroyed Viaduct

Course of Blockships

True North

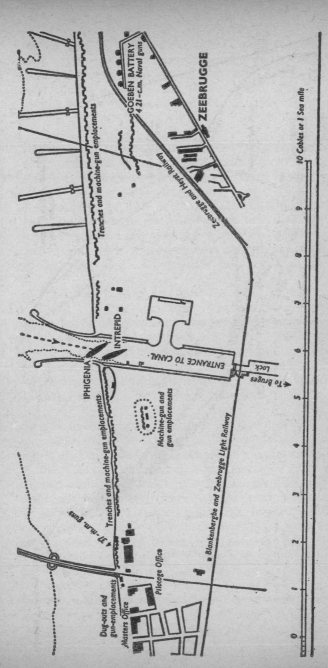

GOEBEN BATTERY
4 21-c.m. Naval guns

ZEEBRUGGE

Zeebrugge and Heyst Railway

Trenches and machine-gun emplacements

INTREPID

IPHIGENIA

ENTRANCE TO CANAL

Lock

To Bruges

Trenches and machine-gun emplacements.

Machine-gun and gun emplacements

Blankenberghe and Zeebrugge Light Railway

37-m.m. guns

Trenches and machine-gun emplacements.

Pilotage Office

Dug-outs and gun-emplacements

Masters Office

0  1  2  3  4  5  6  7  8  9  10 Cables or 1 Sea mile

Immediate Plan of British Attack on Zeebrugge, April 22-23, 1918
with the object of blocking Zeebrugge Canal

home. Bitter disappointment and frustration was felt by all on board, but a detached observer could with justice have pointed out that at least her casualty list—in numbers—was not excessive: the quality of the gallantry displayed by Bradford, Hawkins and Hallihan was, of course, unmeasurable.

This cold comfort did not last long.

As she turned away northwards she steamed directly under a salvo of falling shot from shore batteries. There was a violent explosion and *Iris* disappeared behind a vast sheet of flame: when next seen she was lurching away to starboard with the port end of the bridge a smashed ruin, and flames shooting up around the conning positions. Aboard, shock from the stunning violence of the disaster held momentary sway, then men rushed up from below to deal with the fire. They were led by Lieutenant Oscar Henderson who brought up hoses to deal with the flames, but after one look at the bridge he decided that his position was up there.

In the shambles of the control stations he found senior officers Gibbs and Eagles mortally wounded, the navigating officer practically unconscious from loss of blood and the quartermaster desperately trying to bring the ship under control while still fighting off the numbing effects of an 11-inch shell's exploding within ten feet of him.

By now the *Iris* was well off course and circling to starboard—straight into the field of fire of the Mole Extension batteries. The German gunners, denied a target larger than a motor launch for the last fifteen minutes, had witnessed the explosion and had had ample time to prepare their reception. As Henderson rallied the quartermaster, and the navigating officer—Lieutenant George Spencer—willed himself back into a state where he could whisper out a course, *Iris* crossed into the zone of the Mole guns' fire. Immediately the waters erupted around her as 105-mm. and 88-mm. shell crashed through her sides and swept her decks. In seconds, her casualty list rocketed from three to one hundred and fifty—and she was still under fire. One fact alone saved her—Spencer had managed to correct the course during the split second before the shells hammered home. Petty Officer David Smith flung over the helm, and staggering under the repeated blows though she was, *Iris* answered. Slowly she swung around north again, and as she did so, *M.L. 558* under command of Lieutenant-Commander Lionel Chappell came sweeping through the point-blank fire, regardless of her own danger, to cover her in smoke.

The Mole guns still blasted, the fire under the bridge was rapidly getting out of hand and *M.L. 558* was just as subject to the law of averages as any other craft—she could not expect to live much longer in those waters. But aft of the main hatches a cursing, bloody-minded Australian was exhibiting typical disregard for enemy intentions. Acting Artificer-Engineer William Henry Edgar, R.A.N., had arrived on the upper deck and was carrying out necessary repairs to the damaged smoke canisters. As *M.L. 558* swung back for yet another trip through the flames of hell, black smoke suddenly jetted from *Iris*'s stern and she vanished behind her own screens.

Those aboard straightened up with a sigh of relief and *Iris* herself seemed to ride a little easier. Then three more shells from the heavy shore batteries crashed through her decks. Chaos was come again: it was incredible that she did not plunge to the bottom like stone.

Possibly her double hull saved her—but she was desperately hurt, and in the tight confines of her decks the slaughter had been appalling. She was by no means out of danger, even under smoke and limping out of range, for there was still a fire roaring away under her bridge. Incredibly, Henderson was still unhurt, Spencer still conscious and David Smith still at the wheel, steering with one hand while he shone a torch on the compass-needle with the other, blinded by the smoke from the flaming ammunition, which was almost as dense as the Brock screen aft.

Smith looked as though he would last some time longer: Spencer must die if the gods willed, but Henderson's duty was now to organize the fire-party. He threw himself down the bridge ladder and ran around to the foredeck. The solitary survivor of his original volunteers from below was already at work—in fact he had hardly stopped since arriving on deck. Able Seaman F. E. M. Lake had been endeavoring to stifle the fire with buckets of sand and he had received a certain amount of aid from an unlikely source—the terrifying explosions of enemy shell around him had shaken apart the ammunition stacks and the blast had partially blown out the flames, enough to give him a fighting chance.

Now, with the aid of Lieutenant Henderson, the remainder of the conflagration was brought under control, and with the type of courage which earned many a George Cross during World War II, Lake set about sorting out live bombs from the debris and hurling them overboard, some of them disappearing into the sea with a puff of steam and an audible hiss. Disregarding the pain from his blistered hands, Lake then joined Henderson who had taken charge on the bridge (Spencer had collapsed at last, and was dying) and relieved Smith at the wheel. Six hours later he was still there, blackened, dead-tired, but unyielding.

He was in good company—six feet away from him was Signalman Tom Bryant, half-sitting, half-lying in the angle of a bulkhead. Bryant had been on the bridge when it was first hit and was one of the wounded who were quickly carried below to the surgeon. Soon after arrival in the makeshift sick bay, however, he learned that he was the only surviving signalman aboard. Ignoring his injuries, he had himself carried up and placed in a position where he could receive and send the vital messages. He lay there in considerable pain—without morphia, and knowing that both his legs were badly shattered—until finally, in the absence of any other form of relief, unconsciousness mercifully overtook him.

Both Lake and Bryant received the Conspicuous Gallantry Medal: it was, one feels, about the least they deserved.

In the sick bay below, Captain Frank Pocock, M.D., was faced with a fearful task: over a hundred men needed his urgent attention and he had not one skilled man to help him—his entire staff had been wiped out. It was several hours before any relief arrived—a surgeon from the monitor *Erebus*—and during all that time Pocock worked

120

without a second's break, in appalling conditions, at a task which requires the highest degree of mental and spiritual concentration. He was still at it when *Iris* arrived at Dover at 2:45 P.M. the following afternoon. He had been on his feet at the makeshift operating table for thirteen and a half hours.

He deserved his D.S.O.

Valentine Gibbs had died in great pain but indomitable spirit at 9 A.M., and it is reported of him that never once did he inquire as to the extent of his own injuries or of his chances of survival. These were matters of little import: the burning question which he asked over and over again was—had the operation succeeded? He was bitterly disappointed that *Iris* and her men had been prevented from contributing more to the enterprise, and that he himself had not been more successful in helping his lifelong hero, Roger Keyes.

Practically all the men on *Iris* felt like this. The heat and terrors of their recent Calvary had burned away much of their frustration: now they just wanted to know the final results of the enterprise.

"Have we won? Did the blockships get in?"

This was the fundamental question.

# 9

AFTER ZERO hour—at 'D' buoy—the blockships had deliberately steamed at a slower speed than the rest of the convoy: they were due to arrive at the end of the Mole twenty minutes after the *Vindictive,* by which time it was thought that the assault diversion would be at its height.

Leading the blockship flotilla was the *Thetis.* At midnight the men on the bridge could hear the opening thunder of the overture but could see little of the fire and fury due to the slowly approaching smoke screen. Not that they were themselves completely out of danger, for the enemy was under the impression that the action on the Mole was merely the forerunner of a large-scale invasion, and heavy guns of the Friedrichsort and Wuerttemberg Batteries were engaged in putting down a wide barrage some three miles out at sea.

The barrage was nearly half a mile deep and through it *Thetis* led her consorts while those on board endeavored to keep in the forefront of their minds the true but unconvincing dictum that for falling shot there is an enormous area of water to hit, and an incredibly small proportionate target deck. When one is standing on that target deck, however, it does not appear so small: they were all glad when eventually they nosed their way into the smoke screen and the world was reduced to five feet square.

On through the smoke the blockships steamed, and as they approached the Mole, the noise of battle grew. Suddenly they were hailed from *M.L. 558* (the same ship which later saved the stricken *Iris*) and the voice of Captain Ralph Collins, commanding the Zeebrugge M.L.s, shouted a distance and bearing. At twenty minutes past midnight, the smoke suddenly thinned and vanished. Directly before Commander Sneyd's eyes appeared the great masonry buttress of the Mole end and the lighthouse above it, all superbly silhouetted against *Vindictive*'s bursting rockets and the startling, yellow glow of the viaduct explosion. Sneyd put his helm hard over and increased speed, signalling to *Intrepid* and *Iphigenia* to do likewise, and swung around into the sweep of the Mole.

Directly ahead of him lay a barge-boom with a gap at the southern end. Shoreward of the gap lay the buoys of the net defense, and some three-quarters of a mile beyond them—through a witches' brew of fire and smoke—lay the canal entrance. On the Mole Extension the German gunners, having failed to sink *Vindictive* at an average distance of a hundred and twenty-five yards, swung around and opened fire on *Thetis* at less than a hundred: they had learned their lesson—gaping holes opened along *Thetis*'s starboard flank and tons of water flooded inboard. Steam, smoke, fire and tumult spread through the riven hull.

The guns on the foredeck answered to the best of their ability, but there were only three of them left aboard, and the targets were legion. One of these was a gun mounted on the outermost barge but suddenly the smoking barrel canted over, water appeared around its base. Before the gun and water-carriage vanished completely, *Thetis* was past and negotiating other difficulties.

Sneyd endeavored to steer his quivering ship into the gap, but *Thetis*, hammered by the impact of shot and caught by a strong east-flowing set of tide, was swept too far to port. She missed the gap and ploughed through the net defense between the two most northerly buoys— tearing the wire mesh to ribbons—and then, carried by her own momentum, plunged on down towards the canal entrance trailing the wreckage behind her. The Germans on the shore could no longer doubt the true nature of the night's attack; abruptly every gun of the shore batteries which would bear, swung around and added its fire to that of the Mole Extension guns. From near at hand two machine guns raked her decks.

Sneyd gradually edged *Thetis* back into the narrow dredged channel which led to the entrance, but the wire nets were wound around the propeller-shafts: the drag of the long length of tattered metal trailing behind tugged

*Thetis* to port. As her screws checked and threshed, she gradually lost way and sagged back towards the shore. By now steam was jetting blindingly from cut pipes, and smoke and flame erupted solidly from the battered hull. Three hundred yards from the canal entrance, the laboring engines at last brought up solid. Listing with the weight of water in her hold, she grounded on the port side of the main channel.

Still the enemy pumped shell into her, still her guns fired back defiantly. If she would never reach her own intended destination, she had at least attracted sufficient enemy attention upon herself to give her consorts a better chance of reaching theirs. Through the black smoke which engulfed her, a green light shone from her starboard quarter. In obedience to its message *Intrepid* swept by on that side—unhindered by net and undamaged by shellfire.

*Intrepid* seems almost to have been ignored, so intent were the enemy upon the destruction of Commander Sneyd and his ship—but *Thetis* had now the advantages as well as the disadvantages of being stationary, and her three 6-inch guns were still miraculously intact. The blackened, sweating guncrews fed in ammunition, and pounded away indomitably at enemy positions, and when *Iphigenia* in her turn swept past, they sped her on her way with resounding cheers.

Then, incredibly, *Thetis* rose to even greater heights.

Telephonic communication between bridge and engine room had long since been shot away, but soon after *Iphigenia* passed, engineer Lieutenant-Commander Ronald Boddie succeeded in getting the starboard engine free, and to everybody's delight the battered ship started bumping heavily forward. Sneyd was too much of a realist to imagine that they could ever reach the canal entrance, but his ship was capable of one more gloriously impertinent act: he put her helm over and swung her head out into the dredged channel. Over and over veered the pair of girders which jutted like a sprit from her bows, then finally stopped as *Thetis* grounded forward.

Messengers from the bridge hurled themselves along the gangways and down the steel ladders, clearing the ship, ordering the boat-keepers to station, turning on the remaining smoke canisters. The forecastle was a veritable inferno under the fury of an exasperated enemy, and the petty officer in charge of the foremost firing-keys was killed. Sneyd therefore ordered the charges in the hull to be blown from auxiliary position, there was a solid and sustained thump as the bottom blew out—and with magnificent aplomb *Thetis* settled down precisely athwart the main channel.

Her decks were awash, she was practically invisible under clouds of steam and smoke, both Sneyd and his First Lieutenant, F. J. Lambert, were wounded and now collapsing under partial asphyxiation: in this emergency, Acting Lieutenant G. A. Belben took charge and succeeded in getting away the only boat still seaworthy. This was the cutter—and even she was badly holed. Eventually, waterlogged but still afloat, they were found by *M.L. 526* (manned by volunteers for the duty), and the survivors taken aboard.

The first blockship, if not completely successful, had nevertheless made a magnificent contribution to the operation.

For Bonham Carter and the *Intrepid* up to the moment when they steamed through the canal entrance, it is not too much to say that it had been a case of "roses, roses all the way." Heavy shrapnel had been fired at them before they rounded the Mole, their way had been illuminated by several light flares, but all these—as Bonham Carter was later so nonchalantly to dismiss them— "were quite useless to the enemy on account of the smoke screen."

As has been mentioned, *Intrepid* steamed past *Thetis* practically unnoticed and completely unscathed, swung to port as though taking part in summer maneuvers and swept majestically into the canal entrance. She was undoubtedly in a position to reach and ram the lock-gates, but in obedience to the plan, Bonham Carter checked her when they reached the line of the coast, ordered full speed ahead starboard engine and full astern port, and with helm hard a'starboard, swung his ship across the width of the channel. This channel, however, was even less efficiently dredged than had been anticipated, with the result that a ship of *Intrepid*'s length—she was just over a hundred yards from stem to stern—could swing only about ten degrees before hitting the silt on each side. In so limited an arc, it was obviously impossible to gather sufficient momentum to bury both bows and stern in the silt, especially as they were more or less slapping broadside on.

For a few minutes, Bonham Carter worked his engines to try to get around further, at the same time ordering his crew (remember he had 87 of them) into the boats. The smoke-canisters were now belching forth thick clouds, which if they hid *Intrepid* and her crew from the enemy, also hid the enemy and the canal banks from Bonham Carter: he forced his ship further and further around, backing and filling with a shattering disregard of the growing attention the enemy was concentrating on him. When it was obvious that he could swing no further, he rang the alarm gongs to clear the engine rooms, brought the charge-keys to the "ready" position and waited for his crew to get clear.

As he did so, *Iphigenia* suddenly loomed up out of the blank fog which now filled the canal-entrance, collided with *Intrepid*'s port bow and pushed her back off the silt: Bonham Carter blew the charges just in time to sink his ship before she slid completely back into the main axis of the canal. Below, engineer Sub-Lieutenant Meikle, E.R.A.s Smith and Farrell, and stoker Petty Officer Smith were still in the engine room, but fortunately only their feelings were hurt.

So were Bonham Carter's, for much of his careful maneuvering had been nullified by the accident of the collision. However, he had no need to worry: Billyard-Leake, after an entrance into the canal mouth similar to Orpheus's descent into the Underworld, had no intention of abandoning the scene until all gaps had been closed.

As *Intrepid* settled, some of the smoke cleared momentarily. *Iphigenia* backed away and her stem swung north and east.

In comparison with her sister ship, *Iphigenia* had had a

rough passage. Steaming past *Thetis* she had been hit twice, one of the shells cutting a steampipe in the bows. As a result the forepart of the ship was wreathed in thick white clouds. When these cleared, *Iphigenia*'s bows promptly vanished into a drifting smoke screen which effectively cut Billyard-Leake's vision to about three feet, and when the ship emerged from this it was just in time for him to see that they were practically aboard the western pier.

Only by flinging his helm hard over and slamming both engines astern did this extraordinarily competent young officer keep his ship afloat. As it was, she veered to port only just enough to enable her to slide into the canal mouth "more or less scraping along the western bank." She cut sharply between a dredger and a barge, severing the hawser which joined them and pushing the barge up the canal ahead of her. Before she could get clear of this bumping, infuriating menace, she was well into the heart of the hornets' nest stirred up by *Intrepid*. Machine guns hosed *Iphigenia*'s decks, shrapnel burst overhead and whistled between her stacks, and she was engulfed in *Intrepid*'s slowly-drifting smoke screens. Once more Billyard-Leake's vision was cut to a matter of inches.

As the smoke cleared, the collision took place. *Iphigenia* brought up all-standing, hung for a second and then slid slowly backwards, but between *Intrepid*'s bows and the eastern bank was now a gap of some forty yards, and Billyard-Leake knew that it was now up to him to retrieve the position.

He rang engines astern, tugged his ship's bows out of the silt into which they had bounced, and then went ahead again on the same handling as Bonham Carter had used. Like *Intrepid*'s commander, he was forced to back and fill, edging his ship across the width of the canal, with each movement like a motorist trying to park between two trucks. Few motorists, however, have to park their vessels under conditions similar to those which reigned in the canal mouth.

It was now 12:45 A.M. In another five minutes' time, *Daffodil* would sound the recall signal for the men on the Mole. But even if Billyard-Leake had the attention to

127

spare, it was unlikely that he could have heard it through the pandemonium raging about him. At last the enemy had realized the full extent of the blow which had been delivered against them, and could visualize the humiliation they would suffer in the cold light of day: they were out for blood, and that of *Iphigenia*'s captain would do as well as any and better than most.

But if Billyard-Leake was aware of this, he was singularly unconcerned: by now his ship was well across the channel, her bows deep into the silt of the eastern bank, her stern well ashore on the opposite side. He rang the alarm gongs, cleared the engine rooms, blew the charges and sank his ship. When the decks were nearly awash and the majority of his crew aboard the remaining cutter (one had been reduced to matchwood) he descended from the bridge, crossed the deck, stepped over the side and joined them. Hours later, he still—to quote Keyes's words—"might have walked straight out of a military tailor's shop, equipped for the trenches, leather coat, shrapnel helmet all complete, very erect and absolutely unperturbed."

He was just twenty-two years old.

Meanwhile, Bonham Carter had been facing the problems arising from what he euphemistically refers to in his report, as his inability "to get rid of my spare watch of stokers at 'D'." During the run in, excellent employment had been found for these extra hands, passing ammunition and manning one of the foredeck guns, but now their presence was undoubtedly an embarrassment. To evacuate ship there were only two cutters, which would normally accommodate 22 men each, and a skiff into which ten men might be uncomfortably packed.

Part of the problem had already been tackled. By the time Bonham Carter blew *Intrepid*'s charges, one cutter-load was already away. With a freeboard which would have caused raised eyebrows on a canoe-lake, this cutter wallowed out of the canal, across the entire width of the Mole harbor and out into the North Sea, where she was eventually found some miles northeast of the Mole by the destroyer *Whirlwind*, and the men taken aboard.

Since the blockship crews had been specifically told that the best they could hope for was a German prison-camp, those on board this cutter no doubt preferred to risk a hundred and twenty mile row across to England: certainly they were extraordinarily fortunate to be picked up once they had reached the open sea.

Eventually the other cutter was filled until it was obvious that she could take no more, and with Sub-Lieutenant Meikle in charge, pushed off in the direction of the canal entrance where they immediately ran into rescue launch *M.L. 526*, standing in after they had taken aboard the crew of *Thetis*. This left on *Intrepid* the skiff and some sixteen men—not including Bonham Carter, his officers, and various senior members of the Petty Officers' Mess who showed a stubborn determination not to abandon *Intrepid* without their Captain. The skiff left. It pulled out under the stern of the *Iphigenia* and almost immediately came alongside *M.L. 282*, which with *M.L. 526* now constituted the entire rescue force. *M.L. 128* had already broken down and *M.L. 110* had been almost blown out of the water. This meant two rescue launches instead of four—one complete steaming crew extra, plus numerous stowaways.

As the skiff went alongside the starboard bow of *M.L. 282*, *Iphigenia*'s cutter—now holed and almost awash—reached her port bow. Men scrambled up on to the motor launch's foredeck in a never-ending swarm and soon over a hundred men were packed like sardines on a craft which was built to carry fifty at most. The enemy was now well aware of what was happening and machine guns and pom-poms switched their fire from the smoking but now abandoned blockships to the fragile, thin-skinned and virtually unarmed launch. Lieutenant Dean, in command of the launch decided that for the sake of the men now aboard, those still in the *Iphigenia*'s cutter had better stay there; the cutter was roped to the launch's stern which then went slowly astern.

As the M.L. gathered speed and drew away, the enemy fire increased in fury and concentration. On the packed decks the casualty rate was high. Suddenly a brilliant white light flared up from the surface of the water just to

129

seaward of the sunken *Iphigenia*. Once more the enemy switched fire. For the moment, *M.L. 282* enjoyed a respite, but it was not to last long: the white light was a flare fitted to a Carley float—and on the float were Bonham Carter, his first lieutenant, his navigating officer, and his coxswain. They had left the *Intrepid* as soon as the ship was clear below decks. The Carley float had been dropped over the side, and they proceeded to paddle in the direction of the canal entrance. As they were passing under *Iphigenia*'s stern someone accidentally trod on the rescue flare, igniting it. The light attracted a rain of small-arms fire, driving them into the water. The float, with its Holmes Flare still blazing brightly, bobbed slowly away.

Bonham Carter and his party swam on down the canal. The night was dark, the air above was thick with smoke and escaping steam. They were swimming in water lashed by machine-gun bullets and heavily coated with oil; if it caught fire they would be burned to death.

Dean on *M.L. 282* saw the figures in the water and, despite the fact that he was already grossly overloaded, took his M.L. back into the canal. Once more she slowed almost to a complete stop under heavy fire while more survivors of the blockships came aboard over her bows. All except Bonham Carter. He had waited until last ("Actually," he protested, "I was the slowest swimmer"), and was left behind. When Dean put his engines astern under the impression that everyone was aboard, he just managed to grab a trailing rope and was dragged through the water.

Smashed and wrenched by the waves, he was nearing exhaustion when a crewman saw him and shouted to him to hang on. But the pull of the water was too strong. Before the crewman could work his way forward to the bridge, Bonham Carter had reached the end of his endurance. The rope tore through his hands and he watched the M.L. shoot out into the wide area of the harbor. When the pain in his arms had subsided enough for him to move them, he started swimming slowly back towards the eastern pier of the canal entrance.

By the time the deckhand had reached the bridge,

Bonham Carter had been left far behind. By the light of German star-shells, however, Dean could see the dark shape of his head in the water. Once more *M.L. 282* went forward into the canal mouth. Firing at close range, German machine-gunners and riflemen raked the deck, causing many more casualties. By the time Bonham Carter was at last aboard, the packed ranks of men on deck were thinning ominously.

With his steering gear jammed and his leading deck-hand a casualty, Dean coolly worked his ship out under engines, clearing the canal entrance in a long sweep astern which took them across the harbor, and almost into the shadow of the Mole. When they reached a point not far from the wrecked viaduct, he rang his engines ahead. *M.L. 282* picked up speed and proceeded along past the seaplane base, the battered sheds, the torn and scarred enemy destroyers, and under the guns at the end of the Mole extension.

The motor launch was still under fire from rifles and machine guns, and the casualty list mounted inexorably, but the greater danger from the Mole batteries was avoided by keeping so close in to the Mole that the guns could not be depressed sufficiently to fire on them. When they reached and passed the lighthouse, Dean held course so that the guns masked each other until they were out of sight, if not out of range. All this time, *Iphigenia*'s cutter was still bumping alongside at the end of the forward tow and there seems to be a genuine note of regret in Dean's report—as though he was reluctantly parting with an old friend—when he comes to his decision to cut her adrift: all the blockship survivors were now aboard the launch. Then he altered course for the retirement—for the steering was free again and Potter was at the wheel. Dean could now afford to relax enough to take stock of his command and the men aboard her. From the standpoint that it had not been expected that *any* of the blockship crews would be rescued, the position was undeniably first-rate—but from the point of view of immediate, actual circumstance, it left much to be desired. *M.L. 282* was grossly overburdened and of the large number of men aboard, many were dead, some were dying fast and too many would soon join that class if medical aid was not quickly forthcoming.

In addition, one of the after smoke-canisters had exploded. In the resultant fire, damage was caused to the sternpost and decking, and several officers and men (Billyard-Leake and Lieutenant Cory-Wright among them) were partially gassed. Dean was also by no means certain that his engines had not been overstrained, in which case he could shortly expect trouble. Of his original crew, only his engine-room staff were still at their posts: his first lieutenant was badly wounded and his deck crew dead.

He was working out the odds against a safe arrival back at Dover when there was a sudden shout from up in the bows. As he made his way for'ard again, the shout was repeated, then taken up by other voices until they all joined into one vast, swelling cheer. Along the deck, men were struggling to their feet, the badly wounded trying to prop themselves up and pulling at the trousers of the fit men to secure their help, the gassed cases were coughing fitfully and fighting for breath to join in: tears streamed down blackened faces, throats raw from smoke and fire still contributed hoarsely to the excitement.

Then Dean reached the bridge and looked ahead.

Steaming towards them was H.M.S. *Warwick,* the huge silken battle flag at her masthead and Keyes's unmistakable figure on the bridge. By the time they were alongside, Keyes was leaning over the deckrails, and question and answer were shouted across the intervening gap.

The last pieces of the picture fell into place.


"Keyes," related one of the men who had spent the night with him on the bridge of H.M.S. *Warwick,* "really behaved far better than any of us had a right to expect!"

Certainly those like Tomkinson who knew him well, were astonished at the control Keyes had exerted over himself at moments when it was obvious that he really wanted to be right in the thick of the action. During the Dardanelles campaign he had frequently interpreted his duties as Chief of Staff in a far more executive manner than was usually associated with that post, and Campbell, who commanded *Warwick* at Zeebrugge, was fully expecting to be told to take his ship alongside the Mole so that Keyes could join the assault parties, alongside the viaduct so that he could take a hand with the submarines —and finally into the canal so that they could all go ashore and capture a few heavy batteries.

But although it was frequently noticed that Keyes was eyeing the crucial areas rather wistfully, he never lost sight of the conception as a whole. Indeed, there seems to have been a strange feeling in all units that his was the guiding hand which steered not only the expedition but each separate individual and craft as well. Keyes had made the spiritually awkward transition from active to Flag command with unexpected success.

Nevertheless, H.M.S. *Warwick* had not been a mere spectator.

At the time when *Vindictive* was first revealed to the Mole gunners, *Warwick*—with *Phoebe*—was standing off to the west of the Mole as outer guard, and Keyes first exhibited this sudden impressive command by keeping her there despite the thunder of the battle raging only a matter of cables to the east. When sufficient time had elapsed for *Vindictive* to have secured, Keyes quietly directed Campbell to proceed to the Mole end to cover the approach of the blockships. It was while so engaged that they had experienced the only close, personal action of the type in which Keyes revelled.

When the *Warwick* had reached the vicinity of the lighthouse the wind had already done its worst, but it was still freshening and the small craft in the vicinity were constantly exposed as a result. Until the blockships actually arrived, *Warwick* joined in with what can only be described as boyish enthusiasm. Smoke pouring from stacks and canisters, she had wheeled and circled, emerging from her own screens to take occasional pot-shots at the battery, then returning into them or dragging them across some suddenly revealed smaller craft.

While she was so engaged, the blockships swung around the lighthouse and passed in towards the canal. At about the same time the viaduct blew up with a vast sheet of flame. This was sufficient to bring Keyes back to the solid earth of high command—if indeed he had ever left it, for he had remained unusually detached even during the brief moments of exposure to close fire. He told Campbell to return outside the Mole to see how *Vindictive* was faring.

Somehow they missed *Vindictive* in the smoke screens, and eventually ran alongside the Mole well past the position first occupied by *Iris*. It was from this position that Keyes, standing on the compass platform, saw the block-ships all grouped together in the canal mouth. Whether they were in and sunk at this moment was not certain, but Keyes realized that *Vindictive* had served her purpose at about the same time that Carpenter was coming to the same conclusion.

*Warwick* stood off and waited—for Keyes was showing a most praiseworthy disinclination to interfere with the individual responsibilities of his captains—but at about 0110 he did suggest that they approach *Vindictive* in order to signal the desirability of a withdrawal: as *Warwick* approached *Vindictive*'s position, a star-shell suddenly lit up the area and the gallant old cruiser was seen to be already under way—in fact Campbell had to put *Warwick*'s helm hard over to avoid her as she circled out from the Mole.

They followed for a while to make sure that *Vindictive*'s steaming capabilities were sufficient to take her home, then returned towards the Mole to find and help any of the smaller vessels who needed it. Now the strain on Keyes began to mount to a crisis, for he was still unaware of the success or failure of the operation. *Daffodil* and *Iris* were gone now and the small ships of the smoke patrols were all withdrawing.

Gradually the seas around Zeebrugge were emptying.

Then they saw *M.L. 282* and heard the frantic cheering of the men aboard her. The tiny craft listed heavily as she came alongside and over a hundred men were taken from her, including twenty badly wounded and many dead.

By the time they were all aboard, Keyes knew that two

of the blockships were in the canal and that, as far as could be judged at the moment, the canal was blocked. For the first time in many months, he felt the warm, vitalizing glow of concrete achievement.

# 10

THE LOSSES in craft at Zeebrugge had so far been remarkably small: in fact until practically the last few minutes, two motor launches made up the sum total. One of these had been *M.L. 110,* one of a pair of motor launches charged with the duties of guiding the blockships in by placing flares on each side of the canal entrance. They were to moor just inside the lip of the eastern *estacad*e until the arrival of the blockships, then assist in the rescue of the blockship crews.

The other motor launch of this unit, *M.L. 128,* had developed engine trouble soon after passing 'G' buoy Realizing that he was now faced with a double duty, Lieutenant-Commander Young in *M.L. 110* took his craft on at high speed to give himself the necessary extra time.

They ran out of the smoke screens soon after *Vindictive* had reached the Mole, and the Mole Extension gunners—guns fully loaded—were feeling cheated of their target: *M.L. 110* appeared at the worst possible psychological moment. Three heavy shells caught her almost simultaneously and fairly lifted her out of the water. Although smoke screens were quickly draped over her by every craft in the vicinity, it was obvious that she was doomed. Her captain was mortally wounded, her leading deckhand killed, a spare officer and two men badly wounded: the first lieutenant, Lieutenant G. Bowen, took immediate command and launched the dinghy. The dead and wounded were lowered into it, and the remaining deckhand held her while Bowen went below. A hole was smashed in the launch's hull with an ax and two trays of Lewis-gun ammunition fired through the bottom.

Then the remainder of the crew piled into the dinghy and pulled away. As *M.L. 110* heeled and sank, *M.L. 308* slid alongside the dinghy and took the survivors aboard.

An almost exactly similar fate befell *M.L. 424.*

Her captain and two deckhands were killed as they ran out of the smoke screen, and another deckhand wounded, and the second in command, Lieutenant J. W. Robinson, dealt with the situation with the same efficiency and promptiness as Bowen had displayed. This time the motor launch was destroyed by setting fire to the engine room, and her crew picked up by *M.L. 128*.

When *Vindictive* left the Mole, these were the only vessels to have been sunk by hostile action or the misfortunes of war. Now, however, the expedition was to pay more heavily for their intrusion into enemy-held waters.

The destroyer *North Star,* having followed *Warwick* and *Phoebe* in the first approach to the Mole, had lost them in the smoke screen and for some time took station astern of *Melpomene* and *Morris* in mistake. As the duty of these two ships was to patrol the area immediately adjacent to his own, the *North Star*'s captain, Lieutenant-Commander K. C. Helyar, although slightly puzzled, was not alarmed by the movements of his consorts, which he faithfully copied or complemented as occasion demanded. After all, he believed the flag officer of the expedition to be aboard the leading vessel of this division, and if his own activities were not in accordance with authority's wishes, he had no doubt that he would very quickly be informed of the fact.

He thus continued innocently and expertly as a member of the middle guard patrol until he received a surreptitious and rather plaintive inquiry from the stern of the destroyer immediately ahead, asking who he was and what he thought he was up to.

The mistake discovered, Helyar was in haste to put the matter right. He altered course to one which he hoped would take him down towards the coast, at an angle roughly corresponding to the axis of the Mole, and slightly northwest of it. If he could once pick up *Vindictive* or the end of the Mole, he could navigate from there with accuracy. However, he started from a position far more easterly than he believed, and twenty minutes later narrowly avoided running ashore under the guns of the German "Kanal" battery.

A searchlight was switched on to them from the shore and a torpedo track came straight for them, passing underneath the *North Star* amidships. *North Star* swung briskly around—pausing only long enough to discharge a 21-inch *quid pro quo*—and made out to sea again. As a number of long shadows had been seen jutting from the shore during the turn, Helyar concluded that this must be the Mole causeway and, once out of the searchlight beam, turned back inshore.

These long shadows must, in fact, have been a series of *estacades* or groins which run out into the sea some eight hundred yards east of the canal, so the position of *North Star* was still not correctly established and Helyar was soon putting his helm over again to avoid grounding. However, there was no searchlight to bother him now, only the unmistakable silhouettes of houses uncomfortably close on his port beam. He ran along parallel to the shore until he saw masts and funnels outlined against the sky ahead of him. These, he soon discovered, belonged to the sunken *Thetis*; with the discovery came both mental and physical illumination—for *North Star* was picked up by a searchlight from one of the destroyers moored alongside the Mole.

Without waiting for the nice preliminaries of the first encounter with a searchlight, *North Star* swung around and discharged another 21-inch torpedo, but before she could observe the results, batteries ashore and on the Mole opened fire. It was now well past 0100 and *North Star* continued her swing to starboard, picking up speed as she did so until she was racing northwestwards, parallel to and inside the sweep of the Mole. There must have been four enemy vessels moored alongside the Mole altogether, including the one at which she had already fired, and with a fine impartiality *North Star* distributed her remaining torpedoes among them as she tore past.

But there was still the Mole Extension battery to pass—and the barge-boom. She avoided the latter by swinging sufficiently south, but as she came abreast of the lighthouse, the Mole gunners—who had had enough practice by now—at last justified their existence: two salvoes hit her at a range of less than two hundred yards in engine- and boiler-rooms respectively. The boilers blew up, the engines became a tangled steel mass, and *North*

*Star* eventually slid to a steaming, spluttering halt some four hundred yards north of the Mole.

Once more the Mole Extension battery swung around, with the prospect of wreaking vengeance on a helpless—and now stationary—victim.

*North Star* was saved from immediate destruction by her sister-ship, *Phoebe*.

Those aboard the destroyer *Phoebe* had spent an agonizing night: they would have liked to go in and help their hard-pressed comrades but duty demanded that they stand outside and await an opportunity which was unlikely to come. The only relief had come at about forty minutes past midnight, when they heard shouts for help to the northwest.

After a short search, they found the laboring picket-boat with the crew of *C 3* aboard, and her they relieved of the wounded, thus providing work and distraction for the medical staff at least. *Phoebe* then resumed her slow and patient beat to north of the Mole, steaming to and fro in an exact but solitary station.

Then at 0125, her captain—Lieutenant-Commander H. E. Gore-Langton—saw *North Star* shoot out past the lighthouse like a cat out of a bag. With an understandable sense of companionship *Phoebe* went after her. As *Phoebe*'s speed grew, however, *North Star*'s fell off ominously and by the time *Phoebe* was within two hundred yards it was only too obvious why. As if to dispel any lingering doubts, the beam of a searchlight picked out the wounded ship and three of the Mole Extension guns sent an irregular but vicious salvo screaming into her hull.

Gore-Langton immediately altered course to swing his ship across between *North Star* and the Mole, *Phoebe*'s starboard battery barking defiantly, and smoke belching from her funnels and canisters. *North Star* was soon in a thick and completely opaque screen and *Phoebe* swept in close alongside, then on across her bows to take a towing-wire inboard. A few seconds of inquiry and answer shouted across the decks were sufficient to give Gore-Langton a fairly accurate idea of conditions aboard his consort, then slowly he went ahead on one engine, trying

139

to bring his own vessel on the same axis as *North Star*.

The wind—still playing such a vital and fickle part in the night's operation—now freshened, blew the smoke screen across the slowly-maneuvering ships, and at the crucial moment swung *North Star*'s head away.

The tow parted.

*Phoebe* circled to starboard and came in again, but by now both ships were caught in a web of searchlights, and to complete the full illumination star-shell burst overhead like fireworks at a Chinese wedding. Then the shore batteries joined in: at one moment there must have been over ten tons of hurtling metal converging on them and although, incredibly, most of it landed in the sea, both vessels took far too much punishment for either of them to last through a great deal more like it.

One of the minor but potentially fatal accidents suffered by *Phobe* at this time was the severing of her siren-lanyard by splinters. For the next few vital minutes the smoke screens she had managed to lay were unavailing, for the Mole gunners at least could fire at the unremitting shriek she emitted. Alongside the *North Star* now, the crew of the *Phoebe* took in bracing-wires to enable both ships to move out of immediate danger side by side before trying to pass another tow, but luck was with the Germans and a single shell ploughed along the deckrails between them, cutting the wires and exploding on *North Star*'s foredeck to blow her capstan overboard. Before the two ships veered apart, Gore-Langton had time to shout across the Helyar to abandon ship.

*Phoebe* now lay off—still between North Star and the guns, and making smoke again—while *North Star*'s boats were lowered and her Carley floats dropped over the side, followed by members of her crew. *Phoebe* lowered her whaler to help, but the shore guns were still firing and the two ships had not drifted far from the spot where the enemy guns had first registered. *North Star*'s motor-dinghy was capsized by blast and her crew lost—though later it was discovered that they were lost to the enemy, not to the sea, for they were picked up the following morning and incarcerated in convict cells ashore, with other prisoners taken on the Mole.

While her whaler was collecting men from the sea, *Phoebe* slowly circled her stricken sister, still pouring out smoke in an effort to protect her—and indeed it is possible she had some success, for the fire seemed to be slackening. It fell off so much, in fact, that hopes arose in the breasts of many that after all *North Star* could still be salvaged. Gore-Langton, willing to take any chance offered, took his ship gently alongside and once more began the tricky business of making fast.

Then the shore batteries took a hand again and 8-inch shells crashed through *North Star*'s decks: the bracing-wires were cut once more and *North Star* took an alarming and decisive list to starboard. There could be no doubt about it now, *North Star* was doomed. The remaining officers and crew jumped the gap and boarded *Phoebe*. When it seemed evident that there was no one left alive on the sinking ship, *Phoebe* drew away—and the figure of another survivor was seen to come out on to the now dangerously canting deck.

Once more *Phoebe* went in close, the deckhands holding out their arms to the lone figure and shouting to him to jump. At the crucial moment, when he was actually running forward for his jump, a shell burst beside him. Although for a fraction of a second he was seen in midair against the flame of the explosion, he never landed on *Phoebe*'s deck. It was never known who he was: his name is lost among those who died with their ship.

*Phoebe* slid on past the length of the riddled hulk and, when clear of her, turned to bring her torpedo-tubes to bear and thus ensure that *North Star* went to the bottom. As she turned, another salvo plunged into the water alongside. By the time the smoke and steam had cleared, *North Star* had disappeared. It was by no means certain that she had sunk, but both Helyar and Gore-Langton were sure she could not last long, and, in the circumstances, for *Phoebe* to remain in the area any longer was to expose both herself and the crews of *C 3* and *North Star* to needless danger.

She shaped course out into the night. The time was 0225: an hour had passed since *Phoebe* first went to the assistance of her mortally-wounded sister.

141

Months later, the wreck of *North Star* was located on the sea-bottom less than a mile northeast of the Mole lighthouse.

As was to be expected, the story of the C.M.B.s at Zeebrugge contains elements of high tragedy and sometimes even higher comedy—but there is nothing of monotony in any of the reports. Take, for example, the night's activities of Sub-Lieutenant Cedric R. L. Outhwaite, R.N.V.R., who commanded *C.M.B. 5*.

The expedition did not start at all well for *C.M.B. 5*. Very shortly after leaving harbor she developed a red-hot piston, and all on board knew that both common sense and Standing Orders demanded an instant return to harbor. The chances of a responsible senior engineer officer allowing them to put to sea again being somewhat remote, however, Outhwaite instead persuaded a friendly patrol craft to allow them to tie up alongside while the inlet-cage to the faulty cylinder was slipped off, oil injected into the still-glowing pot, and the cylinder cut out.

With the pious hope that this unorthodox treatment would at least keep the engine going until they reached Zeebrugge, and an apparently well-founded belief in his ability to talk his way out of the trouble which would await him if it also brought them back, Sub-Lieutenant Outhwaite took his craft on to join the main force, taking care to remain far enough from the larger members of the fleet to ensure that no responsible officer heard the syncopated beat of his engines.

With *C.M.B. 7*, he arrived off the end of the Mole some five minutes before midnight and together they swung around abeam of the lighthouse intending to find the gap between the barge-boom and the net. At this juncture, however, Outhwaite—an opportunist to the core—spotted the unmistakable outline of a destroyer slipping away to the northeastward and had sufficient faith in both General Instructions for the operation, and his own judgment, to leap to the conclusion that it must be an enemy craft.

As it happened, Outhwaite's instructions were "to attack enemy destroyers . . ." and only a hidebound purist would insist that the rest of the sentence, reading

142

". . . secured to the inner side of the Mole" was an integral or even important part of those instructions. *C.M.B. 5* swung smartly around and a course was set, "aiming—" and this is quoted verbatim from Outhwaite's report— "for a collision with the enemy destroyer."

In the face of the disarming awfulness of some of the statements in this document, one begins to wonder if there is not, after all, some queer, Alice-in-Wonderland strain of logic running through it all: perhaps there was some subconscious desire to get rid of the weighty, court-martial sized evidence rattling itself to jagged pieces inside the cylinder casings. If so, the ruse did not work, for the enemy destroyer—not surprisingly—must have heard his engines and directed upon him first a searchlight, then machine guns, then multiple pom-poms and finally the port battery of 3.5's. For good measure at least two of the Mole Battery guns joined in, and Outhwaite, who catalogs these anti-*C.M.B. 5* measures with a certain petulance, was forced to the conclusion that his chances of reaching the destroyer in sufficient shape to damage her by ramming, were slight.

He therefore fired a torpedo at her at a range of 650 yards, then turned to starboard to avoid the more pressing attentions of the Mole Battery. He was thus unable to observe what damage was inflicted, "but," he offers hopefully, "two minutes after the enemy was torpedoed [*sic*], the searchlight was seen to go out."

He then proceeded east as fast as his battered engines would permit in order to reinforce the eastern smoke screen. This was strictly in accordance with orders and he certainly put in an appearance in that patrol area—but there was little action in the vicinity, and he was soon back in the more tumultuous waters by the Mole. By this time, however, it was becoming increasingly evident that if something wasn't soon done to relieve the strain on the faulty piston and connecting-rods, they would come out through the side of the block—if not actually up onto the bridge beside him.

*C.M.B. 5* went home—and doubtless Sub-Lieutenant Outhwaite faced the future with the youthful philosophy that whatever they did to him now, they couldn't take St. George's Night away.

Then it was discovered that an enemy destroyer *was* torpedoed and badly damaged at a time and place coinciding with those in his report. So the senior engineer officer tore up his evidence and Keyes recommended the gallant sub-lieutenant for a decoration, which—in time—he received.

But Outhwaite's name does not appear in the list of officers recommended for promotion.

The name of Lieutenant Welman, in charge of the C.M.B.s, does appear in this list, and the name of his *confrère* in Unit V—Lieutenant J. C. Annesley—would have done so if he had been in physical shape to accept promotion: they were both admitted to the Distinguished Service Order and few men can have earned the honor as grimly or as steadfastly as they did.

Unit V provided the smoke screens which were to blind the Mole Extension batteries and the lighthouse. Even the cold officialese of the operational instructions could not hide the almost suicidal nature of the risks these craft had to run in order simply to arrive at their patrol area. Once there, the risks increased every minute, and all the time the assault craft remained alongside the Mole, Unit V remained in station.

"Smoke floats," said the order, "will be laid at first to seaward of the Mole Extension battery, and within fifty yards. . . . When the *Vindictive* is in position and before the arrival of the blockships, the same action will be taken on the inner side of the Mole."

And despite the change of wind, the lack of opportunity for the assault parties to put the Mole guns out of action, or the barrage laid down by the German shore batteries—irrespective of the lives of their own men—C.M.B.s *22B* and *22C* carried out their instructions to the letter.

Machine-gun bullets ploughed up their decks, pompoms smashed away the windshields, heavy shell exploded alongside and lifted them out of the water until they were level with the Mole itself—still they weaved backwards and forwards, laying and replacing smoke floats,

144

dragging screens between the guns and the bigger ships. Their engines shrilled and whined as the props came out of the sea, the flimsy hulls shuddered under the weight of water flung over them and splintered under the hail of bullets—but somehow they kept afloat.

But the price was high.

As Annesley's deckhands were shot down, the mechanics left the faithful engines to Fate and the luck of the navy, and came up to take their places; as they were shot down, Annesley's duties grew. By the time he was hit, the entire crew of his C.M.B. were casualties; they clubbed together with their remaining sound limbs to keep the craft at her station. One man's sound hand held the wheel as he lay beneath it, another's managed the throttle with its possessor propped against the housing: and Annesley's eyes and brain coordinated and kept them going.

Welman was not hit. His was the over-all command of the C.M.B. flotilla and his handling of *C.M.B 22B* that night demonstrated a superb expertness. His craft seemed to become a living, thinking entity under his command, apparently able to divine the next fall of enemy shot before it arrived and to mask the enemy guns before the gunners themselves had brought their weapons to bear. He was never out of small-arms range of the Mole guns and there were several occasions, despite the uproar, when he heard—and anticipated—the orders shouted by the German officers to their harassed but nevertheless efficient men.

Lieutenant D. E. J. Macvean commanded *C.M.B. 16A,* with a patrol area off Blankenberghe Harbor and designs upon enemy craft incautious enough to proceed out from it. He was delayed in arrival at his position by slight engine trouble during which he drifted somewhat off course, and being an efficient and clearsighted officer, he deliberately steered eastward for the Mole in order to establish a basic accuracy. He arrived just in time to save *Iris* and *Daffodil* from destruction when their smoke screen was dissipated by the change of wind, but having cloaked them for the most crucial part of their run-in, Macvean handed them over to one of the eastern patrol motor launches and picked up speed for Blankenberghe.

Once again he was forced off course, this time by the viaduct explosion and the wide area which was liberally and rather dangerously sprinkled with falling debris. By the time he was out of trouble he had again lost position. Now, however—while he was easing up to find a checkpoint—occurred one of those happy events which apparently smooth the path of the deserving officer.

A battery of 4.1-inch guns on the coast opened fire on him, "the flash of which fortunately enabled me to locate my position accurately." And if he was still in any doubt about it, one gathers from his report that the enemy was anxious to set his mind at rest. With full illumination—searchlight, star-shell and Gatling—Macvean proceeded delicately about his business and laid his first smoke floats close under the western lip of the harbor: he then retired out to sea and the lights went out.

Not for long, however: his debt to the enemy was soon to be increased, for he was replacing one of his sunken smoke floats when he observed an occulting light inshore. Assuming this to be a moored buoy he made towards it with the object of sinking it but was once more fired upon by an enemy three-pounder. In the resultant pause for maneuver and reflection he saw that the occulting light was ashore: only an abrupt change of helm saved him from grounding. His tribute to enemy cooperation in this matter is all the more graceful for being implied rather than actually written in his report, and presumably it is tact alone which caused Macvean to omit any mention of the fact that not all the enemy fire directed at him passed innocuously overhead.

Quite a lot of it found its mark in *C.M.B. 16*'s hull —but not, praise be, on Lieutenant Macvean or his crew.

But it was a young gentleman named Leslie Robert Blake—Acting Sub-Lieutenant, R.N.R.—who really carried off the C.M.B. plan for the night's work.

He commanded *C.M.B. 7*—the one which accompanied the enterprising Mr. Outhwaite as far as the Mole lighthouse, and then carried on with the allocated duties of

Unit H while his colleague went off on his hiccoughing engines to ram the destroyer.

Like Lieutenant Macvean, Blake is determined that the German forces shall receive due credit for their apparently never-failing cooperation.

"On arrival abeam of Mole," he says, "closed harbor boom and, with the help of enemy star-shell, followed it down until an opening was observed close inshore."

Here—for he was evidently of a somewhat deliberate turn of mind—he de-clutched his engines and idled gently through the gap at a speed which would allow him thoroughly to survey the scene and choose his target with deliberation. He was handicapped by drifting smoke —although for the moment he offers no explanation of its presence. However, "Enemy star-shell northwest of Mole silhouetted an enemy destroyer apparently secured to Mole," he continues, once more giving credit where was due. "I then proceeded to work up to a speed of 30 knots and fired a torpedo at a range of about six hundred yards, point of aim amidships."

Then he stopped.

In the middle of Zeebrugge harbor, less than half a mile from a ship at which he had just discharged nearly a ton of high explosive and to all intents and purposes encircled by hostile—and we now discover, extremely active—guns, he stopped his craft to observe results. Having remarked with due and sober satisfaction a heavy explosion just below the forebridge of his victim, Sub-Lieutenant Blake then turned to port to take station eastward and make smoke screen as ordered—and it is here that the first dissonant note in the report makes itself faintly heard.

"During all this time," he mentions casually, "I was heavily fired upon by machine guns on Mole and heavy batteries to eastward of the canal entrance."

He was also subjected to considerable chivvying by enemy small craft, who chased him across the width of the harbor and eventually forced him under the pom-poms of a bucket-dredger moored to northeastward of the canal.

"Speed," he states blandly, "was now increased to 20 knots. . . ."

And heading rapidly for the gap in the boom, *C.M.B.* 7 ran full tilt into a large and solid buoy.

"Speed," reiterates Blake with hardly a pause for breath, "was now increased to 32 knots in order to lift the damaged hull out of the water."

Like a speed-boat at a seaside resort, *C.M.B.* 7 careered off along the Belgian coast and within minutes was risking internment in Dutch territorial waters. As it was obvious that he could perform no useful task unless he could occasionally vary his speed, he rightly decided that his best course would be to make for Dunkirk, so he swung around and raced back down the coast—past the hornets' nest at Zeebrugge and straight into the one now angrily swarming off Ostend. Once well in the heart of things, Blake stopped engines again in order to examine and repair an oil gland which—not surprisingly—had burst under the pressure.

Finding that his mechanics were losing the race between the completed repair and the flooding of his command through the perforated bows, he resigned himself to the inevitable—and "fired two Very lights in order to attract attention."

There must be a jovial, rotund, laughing deity—a brother of Bacchus perhaps—who looks after people like Blake. The flares from his Very pistol had hardly hissed down into the sea, before H.M.S. *Faulknor*—with Commodore Lynes aboard—was alongside, inquiring rather crisply after the health of the person responsible. After a few avuncular admonitions, *Faulknor* pushed off and the destroyer *Tetrarch* arrived to take the boat in short tow. And so, dangling almost vertically from *Tetrarch*'s stern, with Sub-Lieutenant Blake still proudly in command, *C.M.B.* 7 arrived at Dunkirk.

Opinions were divided upon what should be done about young Blake—there were some interesting suggestions from the bridge of H.M.S. *Faulknor*—but he eventually got a D.S.C.

And nobody grudged it to him.

# 11

By DAYBREAK on the morning of April 23rd, most of the vessels of the Zeebrugge operations were well on their way home. Many had rendezvoused at the Thornton Ridge Bank, but there being no sign of an enemy fleet attack to be met in force, made their separate ways on to Dover or Dunkirk. The destroyers hung back as escorts to *Iris,* with Commodore Boyle deliberately keeping the *Attentive* force as rear screen.

The destroyers generally—with the exception of *Phoebe* and her tragic sister—had not had a particularly exciting or perilous time: a star-shell had fallen on *Myngs*'s foredeck very early in the proceedings, and shortly afterwards a smoke canister exploded with most uncomfortable consequences for the bridge and upper deck personnel. Beyond these slight contretemps, the work of the larger vessels at Zeebrugge had been almost routine patrols, for their presence in the expedition had been as shields against perils which did not appear.

At one time the destroyer *Mansfield* thought she had discovered a marauding U-boat and fired a round of 4-inch and several small-caliber bullets at the submarine before frantic signals disclosed that it was, in fact, the errant *C 1.*

The story of the missing submarine is one of unadulterated bad luck: the tow (from the *Mansfield* as it happened) had parted soon after passing 'C' buoy, in similar circumstances to those which overtook the picket-boat: a stern sea threw unequal strains on the hawser and after much lurching and bucking, *C 1* yawed widely and the wire rope snapped. Lieutenant Newbold immediately started up his engines and proceeded at eight and a half knots towards the place where the tow should have been dropped and the vessels of Unit K assembled, before setting out for the viaduct.

Shortly afterwards he suddenly realized that an unknown length of hawser was dragging from his bows and if it was long enough to reach the propellers it might well wrap itself around the shaft. He stopped engines, slid to a halt and his first lieutenant, Lieutenant F. A. Beyford, went forward to investigate. The swell was still proving awkward and Beyford was washed overboard, but with no fatal results for he recovered himself and returned to the conning tower, wet but undaunted, having released the offending rope.

*C 1* proceeded at nine knots.

It was ten minutes before midnight when they arrived at the proposed assembly point. Course was set to take them along *C 3*'s path, but shortly after this the destroyers were seen, the episode of the mistaken identity took place and she was fired upon by *Mansfield*. By the time mutual recognition had taken place, *C 1* was twenty minutes behind scheduled time and on the fringe of the operational area: to Lieutenant Newbold it seemed that if he went on he ran considerable risk of arriving at the viaduct too late to be of use, but quite possibly in time to butt in and wreck the enterprise.

None of the destroyers could give him any news, for their screening duties kept them out of touch with main events. At twenty minutes past midnight the flash from the viaduct was seen, but once again the lack of the anticipated thunder of the explosion led to doubts as to its actual cause; *C 1* cruised eastward and waited.

Half an hour after the time when *C 3* should have exploded, Newbold decided that the area ought now to be sufficiently free of raiding craft for him to be able to proceed towards the viaduct without risking collision with one of them and resultant obliteration for all as his own charges blew up. He trimmed down until the conning tower was awash and made south towards the coast. When land was sighted ahead, he altered course east and steered for the viaduct. He had reached a point approximately a mile and a half from the Mole, when he recognized *Vindictive* about three miles away, retiring rapidly on a northwesterly course.

"I then found it very difficult to decide upon the best

150

action," reads Newbold's report, "and concluded as follows: *Vindictive* by her early retirement—probably twenty minutes before I sighted her—must have failed in her operation. The wind was then off the land: it was possible that the blockships had also retired, probably meaning that the operation would again have to be carried out with a more favorable wind. I therefore considered that I should best act in the spirit of the operation by retiring."

This he did, arriving at Dover at twenty-five minutes past noon on St. George's Day. His first act upon finding out the true state of affairs was to submit to Keyes the proposition that *C 1* should be used for some other form of demolition in enemy waters, and that he and his crew should be granted permission to carry it out. Throughout the entire frustrating night, he had acted with commendable prudence, but to Newbold that was cold comfort.

*Vindictive* arrived back in Dover harbor shortly after 0800 to a tumultuous welcome only dimmed by the endless stream of wounded carried from her decks to the waiting ambulances. Over two hundred of those who sailed on her went to hospital and another sixty had passed beyond medical help. During the next few days this last number was unhappily to increase.

At 1 P.M. *Daffodil* arrived home in tow of *Trident,* and just before three o'clock poor *Iris* limped in—it had been impossible to tow her, due to flooding in the forward compartments. By four o'clock, all who were to come home had arrived—or were at any rate in friendly hands; the reports were in and the accounting began, for higher authority was requesting details. One of the first signals to go on the air was, in fact, of German origin, and its interception provided great satisfaction at Fleet House. It read: "Until further notice, the canal entrance at Zeebrugge is blocked at low water and obstructed at high water. U-boats will use alternative ports."

Other messages passed through Fleet House during the day. One was from Buckingham Palace announcing that His Majesty had been pleased to appoint Vice-Admiral Keyes a Knight Commander of the Bath, and upon the new Knight Commander's most urgent representations, it was followed by another from the same source, granting the Distinguished Service Cross to Dean's second-in-command, Keith Wright, and a bar to the one already possessed by Sub-Lieutenant Lloyd. Both these young officers had been hurt and were not expected to live—the vast majority of Lloyd's blood was soaked into *Iphigenia*'s ensign, which he had so proudly brought away with him and then, pathetically, seen used as a bandage to staunch his own disastrous wounds. He was to die, but solaced by the news of the award; Wright improved from the moment he was told of the Royal interest and decree, and was to live to wear his decoration.

During the morning Commodore Lynes telephoned from Dunkirk. His news was a temporary dampener; the attack at Ostend had failed. But even in that first summary of the operation it was obvious that the basic plan had been sound. It had been defeated by two, possibly three contributory factors and one of these had been atrociously bad luck. For the rest of the day, Keyes, although he had a thousand tasks to perform—most of them gratifying—carried them out with an air of faint preoccupation.

He hated to leave a job unfinished.

"I am of the opinion," states the report forwarded by Lieutenant-Commander Hardy, Captain of the *Sirius* at Ostend, "that the enemy were prepared for either an attempt to land or to block the entrance, as the whole land appeared to be lined with machine guns!"

There is much to support this opinion—especially when the disappearance of *C.M.B. 33* on the night of April 11th is borne in mind. Yet if Ostend was ready and waiting for the attack, how was it that such complete surprise was obtained at Zeebrugge—where it was later discovered that most of the naval officers were ashore attending a party? The jealousy which existed between certain German organizations during the Second World War is both acknowledged and understood, but the only explanation on the Belgian coast in 1918 would appear to be one of uncertainty: perhaps the Ostend commander was unwilling to risk the derision which might have

152

been directed at him, had all the coastal defenses been stood to from Nieuport to Knokke on April 22—and no attack developed.

But it certainly seems that one was expected that night at Ostend, and from the defensive measures taken the enemy seems to have possessed a clear understanding of the methods which were to be used to launch that attack—at least during the preliminary stages.

It will be remembered that in the absence of a protective Mole as at Zeebrugge, the canal entrance at Ostend was to be found by dead reckoning. Captain Douglas and Commander Haselfoot had established exactly the positions of both the Stroombank whistle buoy and a bell buoy off Ostend beach, and worked out courses and speeds which would take the blockships from the first via the second, straight between the *estacades* and into the canal mouth.

The events of the night were finally to show that the work of Douglas and his assistant was commendably accurate: but it was all nullified by that step taken by the enemy which most amply justifies Hardy's contention of preknowledge. At some time during the late afternoon or evening (quite possibly when the attacking forces were actually on their way) the Stroombank whistle buoy was moved some mile and a half to the eastward, and the bell buoy was completely withdrawn.

The convoy under command of Commodore Lynes left Dunkirk at the appointed hour and steamed without mishap towards Ostend. The monitors took up correct positions—some 14,500 yards to seaward and thus outside the area in which the Germans had made their navigational adjustments. The destroyers, too, were unaffected by these alterations, for in order to avoid any chance of putting the blockships off-course, all craft larger than motor launches had strict orders to remain to the northward of the Wenduyne and Nieuport Banks until the blockships had passed.

It was the C.M.B.s who ran into trouble first.

As at Zeebrugge, it was their duty to lay the first of the inshore smoke floats, and the design of the screen was in

153

some ways more complicated than that further east. Between them, the C.M.B.s and the M.L.s were to provide a double line of smoke, parallel with the shore, extending five miles on each side—but not across—the canal entrance. Then from the Stroombank buoy to the bell buoy, they would lay a passage through which the blockships would steam—straight into the canal itself. Such exactitude and stability could hardly be expected from an element only slightly heavier than air and essentially dispersive.

However, the small-craft captains had the self-confidence of their years, and set about the task with all the expertness and imagination they possessed.

*C.M.B. 19* was the first to find the Stroombank buoy. Lieutenant F. C. Harrison was the flotilla commander, and like others that night he blamed his own navigation for not finding the buoy earlier. He placed a calcium light buoy a few yards north of the Stroombank and proceeded S. 60° E. for the bell buoy. Not finding it, and refusing to believe that he could have lost course in such a short distance, he concluded that it had drifted, and laid the second calcium flare in what he considered to be the correct position. He then went further south to find the canal entrance, but by now the shore defenses were wide awake, and searchlights caught and held him in their beams.

He was blinded by these attentions, then baffled by his own twists and turnings to escape from them: as it happened, he *did* find the pier marking the end of the eastern *estacade*—he was the only person even to see the canal entrance that night—but his course between the bell buoy position and the pier had been so erratic that he had no means of checking their relative bearings. After placing flare buoys just off the pier, he retired under heavy machine-gun fire which unfortunately inflicted severe wounds upon his chief motor mechanic, C. M. M. Alexander. He then made out towards Stroombank to await the arrival of *Brilliant* and *Sirius*.

Meanwhile the M.L.s had closed up and were laying the smoke screens with moderate success, hampered by a heavy and continual barrage, probably put down with the aid of aiming marks fixed during the daytime. The

M.L. flotilla commander, Captain I. Hamilton Benn, M.P., found the bell buoy position particularly unhealthy; while in its vicinity he was brilliantly lit up by star-shell and subjected to a continual hail of 3- and 4-inch shell, well laced with pom-pom fire.

Then he too, having seen that the laying of the smoke was proceeding as well as could be expected, retired towards the Stroombank to await the arrival of the blockships at midnight.

It is most probable that at midnight the blockships were in exactly the correct position. There was, of course, no buoy to be seen and now the change of wind, which had so nearly wrecked the Zeebrugge Operation, completed the confusion of the Ostend force.

Commander Godsal, in *Brilliant,* had received an impression that 'G' buoy—where he had parted company from the Zeebrugge force—was somewhat too far to the north, so when the Stroombank failed to make its expected appearance he merely concluded that his course was correct, but that he had still some way to go. He ran through the northern line of smoke, and into the empty box contained by the screens. Here, he considered, the Stroombank must appear—and as it didn't, he put his helm over and steamed cautiously to the east.

Now the wind defeated him. If it had remained constant, the southern smoke screen would by now have drifted over the enemy gun-positions and the shore be exposed: Godsal would have seen the canal entrance fine on his starboard bow. But with the smoke drifting back towards him, augmented by the enemy who put up their own smoke screens in addition to the clouds of cordite fumes from the pounding batteries, the shore was blanked off, and the only objects revealed to him were two C.M.B.s to seaward, and—disastrously—the Stroombank buoy now some way off to the northeast with Hamilton Benn's M.L. cruising impatiently just beyond it.

Commander Godsal's thoughts upon seeing the Stroombank on his port hand instead of well astern, must have been caustic. However, he put his helm over, and with *Sirius* close astern made for the buoy, swinging around

155

it and at last taking up the determined course for, he hoped, the canal entrance.

M.L.s 532 (Hamilton Benn), 283 and 276 took station astern of the blockships, C.M.B 19 bobbed and swerved between them, all around heavy shell from the shore batteries screamed and crashed. Gouts of water were flung over the small craft, and holes appeared in the hulls of the blockships: there was no doubt that the enemy knew exactly where they were and were making every endeavor to sink them.

Much of the fire seemed to be coming from the east, so Hamilton Benn swung off to port to lay smoke. On the starboard side of the blockships Lieutenant Harrison in his C.M.B. was in something of a dilemma. The smoke screens had now drifted far to seaward, and Brilliant, Sirius and her tiny escorts were fully illuminated by practically every searchlight along the Ostend waterfront: it was quite obvious that all aboard these ships were blinded by glare and relying—fatally—on dead reckoning. A smoke screen might give them some slight protection, but it would also blind them even more: operational requirements come before safety. Brilliant and Sirius ran on through the gauntlet.

Then Godsal heard breakers close on his starboard bow and swung his helm over; but Brilliant was heavy with concrete, and sluggish with the punishment she had been taking during the last fifteen minutes. She touched, swung clear for a second, then ploughed on deep into sand. As Godsal went astern on both engines, Sirius crashed hard into Brilliant's port quarter and rammed her fast aground.

There was nothing Godsal could do now to rectify the matter. He ordered the boats away, switched on his smoke and blew the bottom out of his ship. When he was quite certain that none of his crew were still aboard, he and his first lieutenant, Lieutenant V. A. C. Crutchley, followed over the side and down on to the packed decks of M.L. 276, now close under the stern. The M.L. sheered off and made her way slowly through the shell-pocked waters towards Sirius.

Sirius, according to Lieutenant-Commander Hardy's

graphic report, was already sinking when she rammed *Brilliant*. Four 8-inch shells had found their mark on her hull, and at least twenty 4.1's, but when machine-gun bullets began to whistle close above the forebridge, Hardy's suspicions that something was radically wrong crystallized into certainty. Small-arms fire was to be expected at a certain phase of the operation, it was true—but not yet and not from that direction: nor, judging by the long whine which followed the missiles, from that range.

The poor visibility had necessitated taking his ship close up under *Brilliant*'s stern, with obvious results when *Brilliant* suddenly lost way. Hardy saw his leader check and as a result had put his engines full astern before the actual collision, but tons of water were flooding his forward compartments, and its weight together with that of the concrete took his ship on against the turn of her screws. *Sirius* swung heavily around to starboard and her hull touched bottom. She was aground for good.

Without using her own explosive, *Sirius* had sunk, but for good measure Hardy blew out her bottom just the same.

During the ensuing hour the German gunners fired heavy, medium and light shell, at the two stranded cruisers and everything which approached them, with a prodigality which would have alarmed Ludendorff, to the south, already glancing over his shoulder at his diminishing stockpiles and with his much-vaunted spring offensive grinding to a halt.

Hamilton Benn, returning from his smoke-laying foray to the east, ran straight into one of these shells, just at the moment that he was nosing up against *Brilliant*'s side to help take off her crew. Hours later he was still blaming his own seamanship for the smashed bows and split exhaust pipes which resulted. *M.L. 526* was obviously written off as a rescue-launch. Benn was forced to ask for help—much to his discomfiture—and his command was eventually towed back to Dunkirk. But examination in port revealed several large, jagged pieces of metal easily identified as shell-splinters. The flotilla commander's reputation was saved.

In the event, the majority of *Brilliant*'s crew were taken aboard *M.L. 276*, commanded by Lieutenant Roland Bourke. It had needed four trips alongside the cruiser before Commander Godsal came down the ropes with the assurance that there was no one left aboard. During that time it was patently unhealthy to remain in any one position in the area for longer than a few seconds, and now, with Godsal aboard, Bourke took his command out to sea towards the Stroombank buoy. Later, *M.L. 276* answered Hamilton Benn's SOS and took the flotilla leader in tow, with the result that, heavily burdened as she was, it took nearly five hours to reach No. 2 buoy, off Dunkirk, four of them spent close to an enemy-held coastline.

Nevertheless, when Commodore Lynes eventually returned to port after shepherding other small craft of his squadron home, he was to find that his chief executives had arrived at the office before him. Godsal was there, and so was Crutchley—and Hardy paced the corridor impatiently. They all sang the same song. Ostend *could* be blocked, they claimed, despite the night's events—and they had all armed themselves with cogent arguments, the principle of which was that with the experience they had gained that night they were the best people to carry through a second attempt.

In some ways, Hardy had the best case for he had returned to *Sirius* some time after the area had been abandoned. *C.M.B. 10*, in which he had made the journey, had been quickly seen and hostile shelling immediately recommenced, but the smoke had dispersed and for the first time the position of the sunken blockships could be pin-pointed. They were, as Keyes later informed the Admiralty, some mile and a half east of the canal entrance, hard aground and within 250 yards of a searchlight and heavy machine gun post, 1,000 yards of seven 8-inch gun batteries and two 11-inch gun batteries, and within two miles of the Jacobynessen battery of 15-inch guns.

How any of the blockship crews got away alive remains a mystery as inscrutable as the fate of the *Marie Celeste*.

The men from *Sirius,* including Hardy and his first

lieutenant, Lieutenant E. L. Berthon, D.S.C., had originally been taken off by *M.L. 283* whose captain, Lieutenant-Commander K. R. Hoare, seems to have been possessed of the cool detachment of a post office clerk in a rush hour.

22 April, 1918 (reads his report).
2315.   Arrive Stroombank Whistle Buoy.
2325.   Commence flashing Aldis Lamp N. 20° E. as per orders.
23 April, 1918
0010.   Blockships make Stroombank Whistle Buoy.

His is the only one of a hundred odd reports of the night's action to draw *that* distinction, but later his timetable takes on some of the cold precision of a bank statement.

0025.   *Brilliant* and *Sirius* stop.
0026.   Under way.
0029.   *Brilliant* and *Sirius* aground, going astern in an endeavor to get off.

Neither Hardy nor Godsal mentions this first check in their reports, but the tone of Hoare's document is so assured that here, one feels, is the exact account, unsmudged by the emotions of the moment.

*M.L. 283* did not, of course, immediately proceed alongside *Sirius*; she lay a short distance off until the last embarrassing paroxysms had died, and her captain had made certain that his attentions would be welcomed. Then and then only, when the local disturbances were all due to enemy action and thus beneath notice, did Lieutenant-Commander Hoare take his launch alongside *Sirius* and coolly embark the crew. There was some slight delay right at the end, while Hardy made certain that no one was trapped below, so——

0040.   Leave *Sirius* and stand off, quarter-cable.
0050.   Go alongside port of *Sirius* and take three officers and ratings on board, leaving no one on board.

During this time, *M.L. 283* had also collected 16 men from *Brilliant,* who had put off in the whaler as soon as Godsal had ordered "Boats away," only to have their craft machine gunned into a sieve before they were more than fifty yards clear. There were thus 75 men crowded on to *M.L. 283*'s deck, and although this number was not to compete with the hundred plus which her next of kin was carrying out under the Zeebrugge Mole Extension batteries, it was quite enough, in her captain's opinion, to justify his withdrawal from the scene. *M.L. 276* was obviously dealing competently with the remainder of *Brilliant*'s crew, so *283* circled away and out to sea.

By the time Hoare had reached the Stroombank buoy, however, Hardy and his first lieutenant had counted heads and come to the conclusion that, after all, Engineer-Lieutenant W. R. McLaren and many of his staff were still aboard *Sirius.*

There is no mention anywhere of what Lieutenant-Commander Hoare thought of this apparent carelessness on somebody's part, but he summoned *C.M.B. 10* alongside, and after the matter had been explained to Sub-Lieutenant Clarke in command and that young man had taken his craft rapidly off into the darkness with Hardy and Berthon aboard, *283* proceeded calmly on towards Dunkirk.

In *C.M.B. 10* Hardy and Berthon watched the narrowing gap between themselves and the object of their late responsibilities. About an abandoned and sunken ship there is an air of gaunt desolation—most compelling during the close approach: *Sirius* still cracked and shuddered as her plates cooled and the sea muttered ominously as it explored her guts. Beyond her, *Brilliant* was afire forward, smoke and steam billowing from the foredeck.

But there was no one aboard *Sirius*—at least there was no reply to their calls. Before they had time to climb the dangling davit-ropes and carry out a search, heavy shells were crashing into the sea around them, and Clarke was weaving his agile craft between gigantic waterspouts. There was no reply when they hailed *Brilliant* either, but by that time the clangor of battle had renewed and it was unlikely that they would have heard even were anyone still aboard.

As it happened, both ships had been long abandoned. McLaren and his stokers had left *Sirius* in the whaler and pulled straight out to sea, where they were picked up by *Attentive* thirteen miles from the coast and taken on to Dover.

*C.M.B. 10* drew away from the seething waters around the blockships, circled once, then made swiftly out to sea again. The German guns kept up their fire for some minutes longer, the searchlights waved aimlessly around the sky, then the seas were empty. The batteries muttered like distant thunder into silence and the Belgian coast was still at last.

Operation Z.O. was concluded.

# 12

It took Keyes only a matter of minutes to decide what he intended to do about the Ostend failure, and only a matter of hours to lay down the basic principles of how that decision was to be furthered. He had another talk with Lynes, then several with Godsal and Hardy: then he and the superintendent of the dockyard, Rear-Admiral C. F. Dampier, spent two hours examining *Vindictive*'s wounds. As a result of all these conferences, Keyes sent a message to the Admiralty to the effect that he intended to fit the old cruiser out for a final run across the Channel, and sink her in the canal entrance which *Sirius* and *Brilliant* had so unfortunately failed to find.

Nothing succeeds like success and the Admiralty agreed without demur. Public enthusiasm over the Zeebrugge raid had exceeded anything like it since the relief of Mafeking, and for the first time in months the Government felt safe: let the gallant Vice-Admiral do it again, by all means.

At Dover, the first problem was manpower, for the blockship crews had been sent off on leave, and there were still—day in and day out—the normal routine duties of the Dover Patrol to fulfill. However, men were soon engaged on the task of filling 200 tons of cement and rubble into *Vindictive*'s after magazines and upper bunkers. The tattered outer casings of funnels and housings were ripped off and replaced, the dockyard electric staff worked day and night rewiring the shot-away communications, and their specialists installed a new standard compass.

At Fleet House the conferences were numerous but short and to the point. Commodore Lynes was once again given executive command of the operation and Commander Godsal—almost as a matter of course—assumed command of *Vindictive*.

Godsal, one feels, was the sort of officer who distrusted anything which cloaked or disguised the bare, basic bones of seamanship. He was not an engineer officer, but he knew the routine of his boiler rooms, and the rhythm of his engines spoke as clearly to him as to any oil-caked plumber. He was not an electrician, but he had supervised the leads to the explosive charges in *Brilliant* and then—for he shared Keyes's innate kindness to youth— he went aboard *Intrepid* and *Iphigenia* and walked around with their respective captains, remaking some of the contacts himself with an air of apologetic preoccupation as though he just had to have something to do with his hands.

But he was not apologetic to many—and never to his superiors.

Godsal's officers from *Brilliant* had all volunteered with him for the second attempt, but Keyes, determined that no unnecessary lives should be risked, reduced the operational complement of *Vindictive* to four officers and 39 men. As has been mentioned, one officer extra did sail with the ship "in order to look after his kit," but Godsal's engineer officer, Lieutenant W. Long, had to stand down due to Engineer Lieutenant Bury's stubborn refusal to give up the supervision of *Vindictive*'s boilers; it was, he claimed, unfair to a new captain to expect him to handle his ship successfully in such crucial circumstances if the engines were handled by staff unused to them; and Keyes, who grinned broadly as he listened to this arrant nonsense, finally agreed with due and proper solemnity that Bury and his E.R.A.s should remain.

In order to establish correction of her new compass, *Vindictive* was taken to sea and "swung" by Lieutenant Sir John Alleyn, Navigating Officer of the Monitor *Lord Clive*. A few cursory glances around between decks were sufficient to reveal her transformation into a blockship, and only rudimentary powers of reasoning were needed to divine her destination: Sir John Alleyn arrived outside Keyes's Dover office armed with two years' experience of conning heavy ships between the Ostend sandbanks. He remained as *Vindictive*'s navigating officer.

Godsal's staff was now complete, and his crew were selected from three times the required number of volunteers, all from Chatham and the Dover Patrol.

Due to the Herculean efforts of Admiral Dampier and the Dockyard staff, *Vindictive* was ready within 48 hours of her return from Zeebrugge, but now the weather broke. By the afternoon of April 27th it was obvious that another week of waiting—like the one spent in the Swin—stretched ahead of *Vindictive*'s new crew.

However, ample work was found for everybody in the chance immediately seized to double the striking-power of the attack: the light cruiser *Sappho* had been originally offered as a blockship but was not accepted, and she was now in use as a depot ship up in Southampton Water. With commendable spirit the Admiralty ordered her to be fitted out as Keyes directed, and she was taken over by Lieutenant-Commander Hardy and his officers from *Sirius* who now regarded the April weather conditions with beaming approval, only tempered by a fervent hope that they would improve before the next favorable period.

On the afternoon of May 9th—which was the first possible day of the next period, Keyes and Lynes were both at La Panne as luncheon guests of the King of the Belgians. After a happy and informal meal they all went for a walk among the sand dunes. They had not gone very far when the King drew Keyes to one side and rather shyly offered him the Star of a Grand Officer of the Order of Leopold. It was while thanking His Majesty for this charming gesture that Keyes first became aware of the fact that the wind was shifting offshore.

Within a quarter of an hour the wind was steady from the northeast. With brief apologies Keyes cut short the royal luncheon-party, and he and Lynes tore back to Dunkirk—bearing with them the fervent good wishes of their hosts, to whom Keyes had permitted himself to drop a broad hint on the reason for their precipitate withdrawal.

Among the items of news which awaited Keyes was a report from the Belgian coast patrol that nine German destroyers, which had been sent down to Zeebrugge after

164

the raid, were at sea. If anything was needed to set an edge to Keyes's anticipation, this was it, for he had already arranged that *Warwick,* upon which he would again fly his silken battle-flag, would be escorted by three fast destroyers to shield the northeastern approaches to Ostend. Keyes had long been of the opinion that a flotilla of four well coordinated destroyers was one of the most effective naval units in a night action, and a meeting with a force of over twice that strength would, he felt, give him an excellent opportunity to prove his point.

Lynes could look after Ostend.

The executive signal was sent off within a few minutes of the arrival at Lynes's Dunkirk office, and as *Warwick* arrived back in Dover harbor with Keyes aboard, *Vindictive* and *Sappho* had just emerged on their way across to join Lynes in the Dunkirk Roads. Keyes went aboard *Vindictive,* wished Godsal and his crew good luck, caught sight of the young Sub-Lieutenant Angus MacLachlan in the background but finally accepted his reasons for being aboard with the same air of solemn agreement with which he had confirmed the engine room staff in their appointments.

As he was piped over the side, Keyes turned and looked back at the figures of the officers on *Vindictive*'s quarterdeck. Crutchley stood there, powerful, bearded, solid, indestructible; about Godsal was an unusual air of calm, unworried serenity.

Commodore Lynes hoisted his broad pendant on board H.M.S. *Faulknor* at 2150, in the Dunkirk Roads. There was still an hour and a half before the main blocking force—which he intended to accompany on most of the passage—must weigh anchor, but there were always last minute details to attend to, and if he dealt with these on board ship, then there would be no risk of a delayed departure due to his own absence. His staff consisted of Commander J. L. C. Clarke, D.S.O., Lieutenant-Commander Francis Sandford—especially lent to him for the operation by Keyes—and his intelligence officer, Lieutenant H. F. Witherby.

The spirit in the force he commanded was good. So

that there should be no residual sense of failure from the previous Ostend attempt, Lynes had issued the following memorandum with orders that it was to be read both to and by all personnel under his command:

## OPERATION V.S.

The luck of the wind and the shifting of the buoy—whether by chance or enemy design—foiled our last Ostend blocking enterprise. To have thus failed was the fortune of the war, and need dishearten no one. None could have carried out their duties more admirably than did the Ostend forces on that occasion.

Our new endeavor to block Ostend with *Vindictive* and *Sappho* gives us another chance to equal the splendid success of the Zeebrugge Forces, and I am confident that the spirit and the work of the Force it is now my privilege to command, will achieve its objective this time, if it is to be done.

I wish all hands to realize that the success of our enterprise will have a wide and important influence on the conduct of the whole war.

Signed . . . Hubert Lynes
Commodore, Dunkirk

The passage about the shifting of the buoys was well in the forefront of his thoughts now, for air reconnaissance had revealed the ominous fact that the enemy had removed every buoy in the Ostend approaches that same afternoon. From the point of view of practical navigation this was no more than a minor nuisance, and Lynes had determined that a calcic-phosphide light buoy should be laid as a turning point by *Faulknor* herself, and he, Lynes, would personally ensure that it was in the correct position.

But the timing of the removal of the buoys held an obvious menace when seen in conjunction with previous events. However, there was no point in letting everyone know about it, and with the exception of his staff and the more senior officers, few people were informed.

Keyes knew, and it had obviously sharpened his desire to get to sea with his destroyer flotilla.

The weather could hardly have been better. Wind blew steadily from the northwest and its strength was ideal; the sky was clear, the sea smooth enough for small craft and the barometer was steady. Air cooperation should be possible and the bombardments from offshore monitors present no difficulties at all. In this respect, Operation V.S. differed from Z.O., for there was to be no heavy attack on the shore positions until the moment when the enemy first reacted to the presence of the attacking forces; light, desultory shelling and bombing, which would not strike them as unusual, would take place until the enemy's suspicions were fully and clearly aroused, then everything would open up—heavy monitors, the Handley-Page bombers and the Naval siege guns in front of Dunkirk—and blanket the Ostend waterfront from the Aachen battery in the west to the Jacobynessen beyond Breedene.

The plan was sound and so were the men. Only ill-luck could defeat them.

*Vindictive* and *Sappho* steamed into Dunkirk at 2245, and her steaming-crews went over the side to the last man as a result of strict supervision from the bridge. Fifteen minutes later, the 32nd Division of offshore destroyers left to sweep the way clear, accompanied by the motor launches and followed shortly by the monitors *Prince Eugene, Sir John Moore,* and *M 27.* At 2330, *Vindictive* and *Sappho* weighed anchor and left the Roads, in company with *Faulknor* and escorted by a C.M.B. escort.

Operation V.S. was under way.

Not all of it remained under way for very long—and the defection was serious. Two minutes before midnight, a manhole joint in one of *Sappho*'s boilers blew out; she sagged out of line, there was a brief exchange of signals between her and *Faulknor* which ended in a note of very faint hope, and *Faulknor* hurried after *Vindictive* with Lynes deliberating as to whether he should cancel the operation or not.

If the weather had held after April 23rd, then *Vindictive* would have been sent in alone on the 24th or 25th. *Sappho* therefore was only a supplement—welcome but not essential—and by the time *Faulknor* overtook *Vindictive,* Lynes had resolved his problem: Godsal was wished good luck and told to do his best unaided. *Sappho* by now had turned, and was limping back to Dunkirk with a load of deep disappointment.

At eight minutes past one, Lynes looked thoughtfully around the horizon but made no executive signal, either to his staff or to the rest of his command. As the seconds ticked by, Godsal and his officers first relaxed, then braced themselves for the ordeal ahead. Now there could be no cancellation. 'M' buoy bobbed past, and course was laid for the turning point.

At 0125 *Faulknor*—by now well ahead of *Vindictive* —dropped an Aga buoy four and a half miles northwest of the mouth of the canal, five minutes later the small craft were dispatched towards the shore, and Lynes caught sight of *Vindictive*'s silhouette as she came up from the west. In seven minutes' time she would turn in for Ostend. As *Faulknor* steamed east to join the destroyers *Moorsom, Myngs,* and *Nugent* of the 32nd Division, Lynes may well have reflected that he had done his best, and now he could but hope.

There was as yet no sign of reaction from the enemy although occasionally a routine star-shell would be fired aimlessly up into the night.

At 0135, one searchlight probed uncertainly out to sea: two minutes later *Vindictive* arrived at the Aga buoy and turned in on the final leg. The smoke screens were excellent but Lynes and Godsal were watching the clouds overhead.

By 0143, several searchlights were sweeping across the sky. Lynes issued the executive signal to commence the bombardment. The clicks of the signaller's key had hardly stopped before *Prince Eugene* and the siege guns opened fire, and above the crash of their first salvo could be heard a heavy roar as the Handley-Page bombers came over. But the clouds were thickening; could the aircraft deliver their bombs? Minutes later came the heavy drumrolls, and a part at least of the growing worry was dispersed.

*Vindictive* steamed past the C.M.B. marking the position of the Stroombank buoy at 0145, which left her two miles and 15 minutes still to go, but by now the sky was completely overcast and to the men on the decks of the offshore destroyers there was an oddly familiar look about the flaming onions of the German antiaircraft defences: they were haloed—like English street lamps on a November evening.

There was as yet no reply from shore batteries.

Then at 0148, as though they had been held up in the sky by strings and now the strings were cut, the clouds fell heavily and wetly down upon the surface of the sea, mixed with the hanging smoke screens into a thick, choking blanket which brought visibility down to a few yards, and thus reduced an organized and cohesive striking force into a number of small, isolated units.

Outside the limits of the cloudbank, the two offshore destroyer divisions cruised to seaward, reloaded their guns with star-shell and at 0200, when *Vindictive* and her escort should be almost there, they opened rapid fire above the canal mouth in an attempt to guide in the blinded navigators. As though this was the sign they awaited, the guns of 16 heavy shore batteries sprang to life and laid an almost continuous barrage across the width of the approach. They took a little notice of the high explosive which the destroyer divisions promptly hurled upon them, but not much.

Not enough to make any difference to a target the size of the *Vindictive* anyway, lost in the fog.

At about this time Lieutenant Welman, who had taken charge of the Ostend flotilla—but not of *C.M.B. 22* in which he had sailed—was experiencing considerable difficulty in locating the wrecks of *Brilliant* and *Sirius*, from which position it was intended that he should fire red rockets, as an additional check on navigation and as a possible distraction for enemy attentions away from more crucial areas. The fog descended upon them about two minutes before the time when the sunken blockships should have become visible, and in the cautious hunt which now took place, Welman suspected that *C.M.B 22* was passing between the wrecks and the shore.

This suspicion was confirmed only too quickly by the sound of breakers on the starboard hand, but as they turned to seaward the fog lifted fractionally, and they saw just ahead of them the standing spikes and oblongs of a ship's superstructure. As the C.M.B. steadied towards this ghostly silhouette with the satisfied air of a spaniel at last sighting his quarry, Welman moved towards the Lewis-guns followed quickly by one of the deckhands. The silhouette shifted angle, a searchlight pointed down upon them and the shells of an enemy pom-pom whistled close above the deck housing.

With a crucial operation reaching its climax behind them, the crew of *C.M.B. 22* reacted as one man: the boat shot forward at the enemy like a terrier attacking a bull, four Lewis-guns chattered defiantly from the fore-deck, their tracers ripping along the searchlight beam which promptly went out. By the time the gap had narrowed to two hundred yards, tracer was straddling the forebridge of the torpedo-boat ('A' class), the enemy pom-pom had ceased fire and the boat itself was turning away under the sheer ferocity of the attack. It vanished to eastward—away from Ostend and the operation—with gratifying speed. Welman, who had an acute sense of the passing of time, ordered an abandonment of the search for the wrecks and a return towards the canal mouth. As *C.M.B. 22* proceeded east, dropping smoke floats on the way, uproar broke out ahead of them, climaxed by two loud explosions. There was a brief lull, then the racket started again, growing rapidly in volume and spite.

Lieutenants A. Dayrell-Reed, D.S.O., and A. I. Poland, with their C.M.B.s, were practically the only people not badly affected by the sudden fog, for they were on their final course when it had thickened and blotted everything out. Dayrell-Reed, slightly ahead, merely slackened speed a trifle and ran on, deckhands at the guns, torpedo-coxswain at the tube control. Somewhere to the east machine guns were distantly firing, but the main battle was not yet joined.

The second hand of his watch moved past zero, the engine revolutions mounted, then suddenly the sea in front of them was churned with machine-gun bullets. Dayrell-Reed swung the helm to port: the vague shape of the eastern pier loomed on his starboard side and flame spat from a point near its end. Now the boat surged up to full speed, the deck gunners answered the enemy fire. *C.M.B. 24A* swung around in a long curve to south, then west until they headed straight into the enemy fire now increased by another machine gun and a pom-pom. They held course until they were within 200 yards and wooden splinters were flying from the deck: then there was a sudden, welcome thump from the bows, Dayrell-Reed swung to starboard and, as he circled away, his torpedo slid between the girders under the pier and exploded.

Lieutenant Poland was not so fortunate: everyone who approached the area after *C.M.B. 24A,* steamed into trouble. Nevertheless, Lieutenant Poland combined aggressiveness with accuracy, pressed his attack to within 700 yards, steadied his vessel with deliberation and fired his torpedo. The explosion was seen as far back as the Stroom buoy, which *Vindictive* had just safely passed and on her final spurt towards the canal.

Among *Vindictive*'s escort were two C.M.B.s of the 55-foot class. They were *C.M.B.s 25BD* and *26B* commanded respectively by Lieutenants R. H. McBean and C. F. B. Bowlby, and their duties consisted now in proceeding ahead of their charge until within sight of the canal mouth, whereupon they should drop calcium light buoys and fire flare rockets to burst above the entrance.

In thick fog this was much easier said than done. Through a momentary gap in the fog Lieutenant Bowlby glimpsed the eastern pierhead at the very moment when his boat, his guns and his torpedo-tube pointed exactly at it. He pressed the button, discharged the torpedo and increased speed—with the result that he was directly above his torpedo when it hit either the bottom or a submerged object and exploded, blowing *C.M.B. 26B* several feet up into the air.

She did not sink immediately, but her seams were badly started, her communication system wrecked and her signal and lighting arrangements reduced to chaos. Bowlby turned her away and took her slowly to seaward, with the port engine firing on six cylinders and the starboard engine bone dry. *C.M.B. 26B* made nearly three miles before the engine seized up and she was eventually towed home by H.M.S. *Melpomene*.

Bowlby's partner, however, Lieutenant McBean in *C.M.B. 25B* had remained in closer touch with *Vindictive*. At 0200, when McBean was slightly ahead and to starboard of *Vindictive*'s bows, he suddenly found himself in the middle of the enemy barrage across the canal mouth, and was forced to weave erratically between sudden and gigantic watersprouts.

This meant, of course, that he lost basic bearings. Although he managed surprisingly to keep *Vindictive* on his port quarter, he realized after a while that direction must either have been lost or deliberately changed. *Vindictive* still loomed over his shoulder, but by now they should all have been either in the canal—or ashore. Cautiously McBean ventured ahead and to starboard, with the result that almost immediately *C.M.B. 25BD* was alone in a gray-brown, but shell-shot and extremely noisy night. He circled once without result, but was rewarded upon repeating the maneuver by running into a patch of clearer visibility which suddenly showed him Ostend piers —and *Vindictive* well to east of them.

McBean went after her, firing green Verey lights until they were apparently seen and *Vindictive* started to turn: then he decided that his responsibilities had been amply discharged and *25 BD* opened her throttles and went into battle.

It was 0215 by now and there was not a German gun in the vicinity unloaded or unmanned, and by gunners who were very wide awake and looking for targets. The eastern pier gunners felt the effects of McBean's suddenly released aggressiveness even before they saw his boat, streaking across between the two piers, her Lewis-guns blazing and a torpedo-track already pencilling its line through the water towards them. As the port torpedo had dropped away, McBean swung across towards the western pier, and Sub-Lieutenant G. R. Shaw on the foredeck

Lewis-guns switched his attentions to the new objective, leaving the stern guns to protect their rear.

The western pier was perhaps 400 yards away from them when they started their attack and the guns above the pier had found them before they had gone 50 yards, while enfilading fire came at them from the eastern pier until the port torpedo exploded.

By then they had closed to 250 yards and were racing along a narrow lane between two apparently continuous red tracer-lines: the Lewis-guns were hot, and empty cartridge-cases rattled and bounced on the deck timbers. As the starboard torpedo plunged away, the C.M.B. hung for a second in the recoil, swung slightly away from the pier, then shuddered as a stream of bullets at last hammered into her decks and hull. Chief Motor Mechanic Keel was killed instantly and McBean had to prop himself up in the corner of the deckhouse until Shaw could leave the guns and come aft to take over. McBean was badly but not seriously wounded: but he had good reason for satisfaction.

As *C.M.B. 25 BD* turned away and made out into the darkness, *Vindictive* made her last eight-point turn, then steamed through the canal entrance.

As they had passed the C.M.B. marking the Stroombank buoy, the men on *Vindictive*'s bridge could afford to look down on the spot with a certain amount of wary satisfaction, for if they had sailed from it before on a faulty course, there was no possibility of their doing so this time. So far, except for the breaking-down of the luckless *Sappho*, the expedition had gone well, with no panics or alarms. Engineer Lieutenant Bury and his four E.R.A.s had experienced little trouble with the engines despite the hastily-patched steampipes which had been severely strained by gunfire at Zeebrugge. All was well below, and the 35 men in the engine-room felt that they had done a good job.

So could the 13 men on deck, although their time of greatest trial was still to come. There was as yet no sign of violent reaction to their presence—shrapnel bursts overhead had been both desultory and ill-aimed—and the smoke screens laid by the inshore craft were excellent. This time there *was* a lane running down between eastern and western sections, and at the end of it *Vindictive* would steam out into the open and across the last few cables into the canal. Once through the entrance, Commander Godsal intended to ram her bows hard into the western bank with her stern swinging across to the east, so that the strong, east-flowing tide would help to place her into position and she could be sunk dead across the canal.

Then the fog came down.

For a while Godsal held course, but the situation was too important for anything to be left to luck and he had no intention of running his second ship ashore. He gave orders for engine-revolutions to drop, altered course to westward and cruised along parallel to the shore. Beside him Lieutenant Sir John Alleyn stared grimly ahead through the Navigator's Plague, while Lieutenant Crutchley waited for the moment when his own responsibilities would be called upon after his two brother officers had taken the ship to wherever she was supposed to go. Young MacLachlan was in the after control position.

It was two minutes to two o'clock, the heavy shore batteries were returning the fire of the offshore monitors and flaming onions were crawling up the sky to get at the Handley-Page bombers; but the seas around *Vindictive* were not, as yet, erupting. Godsal ordered a 16-point turn to starboard and they groped their way cautiously back towards the east.

Then at two o'clock the enemy barrage fell out of the sky. Star-shell from the offshore destroyers burst unavailingly above the cloud-cover and soon afterwards McBean's green Very lights were soaring into the air with about the same amount of effect. *Vindictive* made another 16-point turn in the fog and came back westward but still could not find the canal entrance.

Godsal now decided that he must take advantage of the "last resort" arrangements. One more C.M.B still bobbed about close to *Vindictive*—she had been kept there for just such an emergency as this—and a signal was flashed to her. Her young commander, who by now

174

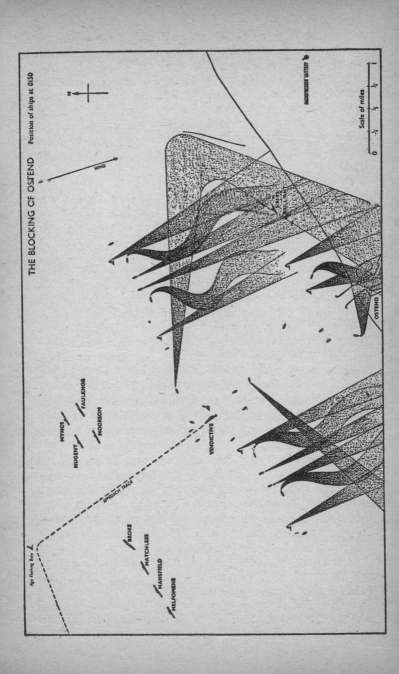

THE BLOCKING OF OSTEND    Position of ships at 0150

N

WIND

MYNGS
NUGENT
FAULKNOR
MOORSOM

Age Flashing Buoy

APPROACH TRACK

VINDICTIVE

BROKE
HATCHLESS
MANSFIELD
MELPOMENE

OSTEND

MONTREASSE BATTERY

Scale of miles.

0    ¼    ½    ¾    1

was expecting it, touched off the fuse of a huge flare, flung it overboard and beat a hasty retreat to seaward. Thirty seconds later a million candlepower flame burst into life just to westward of the canal entrance.

Under normal circumstances this flare would have lit up like day an area of several square miles: as it was, it revealed the canal mouth to the *Vindictive*—just too far abeam for comfort—and the *Vindictive* to the enemy gunners. As the ship wove in as tight a turn as she could manage, the guns found her and began angrily but methodically to smash her upper-works into a shapeless, tangled chaos and the further she progressed into the entrance, the more guns would bear.

By the time *Vindictive* had steadied, Crutchley had passed the order "Preparatory Abandon Ship," in response to which all men who could be spared from below came on deck and lay down beneath torpedo nettings piled along the bulkheads: soon automatic fire was spraying the deck, and machine-gun bullets explored between them like a comb in a spaniel's coat, while heavy shells passed inches above them to wreck the ship's superstructure and topple the standing-gear.

The after-control position was smashed as the ship scraped in close along the western pier, and now Godsal realized that he was in a position exactly similar to the one in which Billyard-Leake had found himself at Zeebrugge 17 days before, except that now there was no sunken *Intrepid* just in front to act as block. *Vindictive* was far too close under the western bank to be able to ram it—to do this she must first move further out into the central channel, and knowing that Sir John Alleyn fully understood the position, Godsal stepped outside the conning tower and gave the order "hard a'starboard" which would bring this about.

Three seconds later a heavy shell crashed against the side of the conning tower with a force which temporarily stunned everyone inside it and severely wounded Sir John Alleyn. When Crutchley recovered, he found *Vindictive* heading across the canal for the eastern pier, the navigating officer practically unconscious, and himself in sole command, for Godsal had been standing at the center of the shell's explosion and was never seen again.

Crutchley's reaction was swift and, in the circumstances, thoroughly understandable. The ship had been committed to a starboard helm by an officer who knew his business; it was sound tactics to follow Godsal's lead and not waste what few seconds were left. He therefore immediately rang port engine full astern to bring *Vindictive*'s head even further around and increase the angle of approach to the pier.

But *Vindictive*'s port propeller had fouled the Zeebrugge Mole when she came away, and little had been done in the way of repairs. There was thus almost no reaction: still heading only slightly off the main axis of the canal, still the target of a dozen heavy guns and twice that number of automatic weapons, the old cruiser plunged across the width of the canal-mouth and at last grounded forward against the eastern pier at an angle of about 25 degrees to the line of the *estacades*. She was quite clear of the central channel, and as Crutchley gave the order "Abandon Ship" and he and Bury blew the charges, the tide was already pressing her even further to one side: she was between the piers, but she was not blocking the entrance.

Ostend harbor and canal were still wide open.

# 13

FOR A. FEW seconds, Lieutenant Crutchley had been
caught, unprepared and half-stunned, on the wrong
foot. Once *Vindictive* was aground, however, he came
into his own, for it had been part of his duties as first
lieutenant to organize the evacuation of the crew. Gigantic, stentorian, he issued his orders and the wounded were
helped over the side, then followed by the remainder.
Petty Officer Reed, who had steered *Vindictive,* carried Sir
John Alleyn across the deck and lowered him into the
skiff where he was later joined by two wounded men.

And still the enemy guns thundered, still the funnels
and upper works clanged and fell under the fire, still
bullets hissed and whined across the deck from machine
guns sited only yards away.

When he was satisfied that everyone who could get
himself over the side had already done so, Crutchley
switched on an electric torch, made a thorough search of
the bridge, then made his way with utter indifference to
the enemy fire slowly along the port side of the ship—
nearest to the pier—meticulously searching for Godsal:
but there was not the tiniest shred of evidence that the
man had ever lived, let alone commanded *Vindictive*. In
the shambles of the after control position, Crutchley
could distinguish no one—young MacLachlan was somewhere in there—and then finding that the after smoke
canisters had not been lit, he carried out the task himself,
except for one float from which he could not extract the
pin.

Then he lowered himself over the side and on to the
deck of *M.L. 254,* still waiting patiently alongside.

He was not a moment too soon. The M.L. had been
badly mauled on her way into the canal and shortly before she had reached *Vindictive* a 6-inch shell had exploded on board, killing the first lieutenant and one deck-

hand, wounding the coxswain and smashing the thigh of her captain, Lieutenant G. H. Drummond, who nevertheless remained at his post, refusing to pull away from *Vindictive* until Crutchley had assured him that there was no one left on board.

Then he put his engines full astern, backed his heavily laden craft out to sea—followed all the way by machine gun and pom-pom fire which cut swathes through the packed decks and inflicted two more wounds upon himself—turned the launch and headed her out to sea. As soon as *M.L. 251* picked up way, however, water poured in through gaping holes in the bows and the forward compartment flooded. Crutchley found himself once more in an unexpected command, for Drummond had at last collapsed over the wheel from loss of blood.

Crutchley sent all spare hands aft, set a baling and pumping party to work—which he led himself—and gave his torch to the nearest man with orders to flash SOS around the half-compass to seaward.

Slowly and desperately *M.L. 254* limped out through the fog. It was now nearly three o'clock, and most of the inshore craft had withdrawn.

But not all: the machine gunners on the piers still had three targets upon which to expend their remaining ammunition.


Hamilton Benn commanded the M.L. flotilla on this occasion as on the previous one. After seeing that *Vindictive* had at last reached the canal entrance, he considered that one of the greatest dangers which threatened her came from the massed and extremely accurate fire of the shore batteries to east of the entrance. In this he was of the same opinion as his opposite number with the C.M.B. flotilla, and he and Lieutenant Welman patrolled as close inshore as their draughts would allow them, laying and constantly renewing the smoke screens as long as their canisters and floats lasted.

In the circumstances, Benn was forced to leave the rescue of the *Vindictive*'s crew to his subordinate captains, and after *Vindictive* had entered the canal he ordered two more M.L.'s, *283* and *128*, to follow and render assistance to *276* and *254,* already detailed as rescue launches.

*M.L. 254,* as has been related, was clear of the canal by three o'clock. *M.L.s 276, 283,* and *128* were still inside, however, and the young officers in command were not as yet satisfied that all living survivors from *Vindictive*'s crew were in safe hands.

Lieutenant Roland Bourke had won distinction during the previous attack, when his craft removed the majority of *Brilliant*'s crew. Now, while Drummond took the majority of *Vindictive*'s crew out through the canal entrance, Bourke broke off the duel he was conducting with the enemy machine gunners and nosed in alongside the sunken blockship.

There were no replies to his shouts—none that could be heard above the uproar created by the other two M.L.s as they strove to distract enemy fire, anyway—so Bourke took his boat out of the canal, while *M.L.s 128* and *283* gave covering fire, slowly retiring to seaward as they did so.

Then Bourke heard cries apparently from somewhere near the center of the canal and turned back. For nearly ten minutes, he prowled cautiously up and down the central channel, straining to hear the cries again above the racket of his own engines and the fire which was now concentrated from all points upon the single target. Finally, almost as a last hope, he took *M.L. 276* back into the shadows under *Vindictive*'s starboard bow. There he found Sir John Alleyn and the two wounded men clinging to the capsized skiff, took them inboard and swung around again for the entrance.

*M.L. 276* was hit by a 6-inch shell on her way out—but it made little noticeable difference to her rather tattered air; in all 55 enemy missiles had found their mark somewhere on her; two of her crew were dead and one wounded, and her engines had suffered as much as her hull. In the event, the fog both saved her and prolonged her trial, for it was 0430 before she was eventually seen by the Monitor *Prince Eugene* and taken in tow.

Although they came away empty, *M.L. 283* and *128* had each played their part in the rescue, holding the enemy machine gunners' attention while the other two M.L.s embarked *Vindictive's* crew: and they both paid for their participation in bullet-scarred planking and shattered windshields. In *M.L. 128* there were casualties as well, for one deckhand had been killed and another wounded. But both craft made their way unaided back to Dunkirk.

"While all this was going on," states Keyes in his *Memoirs,* "I was having a hateful time."

No sign of the nine German destroyers had been seen during the course of the night. After their brief appearance during the afternoon they had apparently retired either to the Heligoland Bight, or else to the shelter of the Zeebrugge Mole.

On the bridge of the *Warwick,* Keyes was possessed by a feeling of crushing impotence which showed in his rigid grip on the bridge rails and his instant, eager reaction to every sound and movement to the east which might possibly have been evidence of the presence of enemy patrols. But no enemy appeared, and as the cannonade continued from Ostend, Keyes experienced the dreadful horrors of high command.

At 0245, fifteen minutes after the time for withdrawal of the small craft from Ostend, Keyes gave orders that *Warwick* and her consorts should patrol westwards, parallel and as close to the shore as their draught would permit. As they approached Ostend, the fog thinned slightly, visibility extended to nearly a mile, and at 0310 they saw a tiny, flickering pinpoint of light.

*Warwick* was speeding in towards it almost before its slow but painful message had been spelled out.

*M.L. 276* was lying stopped with her forecastle almost awash when *Warwick* saw her signal, and the destroyer came alongside very slowly and carefully so as not to upset a most precarious balance.

The huge figure of Crutchley dominated the scene, still baling furiously although rescue was at hand, unwilling to leave even such a sorely battered hulk as *M.L. 276* to her fate. It was still by no means certain that the end of all their troubles was in sight, for the transfer of the

181

wounded was neither a quick nor easy operation, dawn was at hand, both rescued and rescuers were still within range of enemy batteries and on a falling tide in shoal waters.

It was half an hour before the last of the wounded was gently lifted inboard and *Warwick*'s torpedo-lieutenant fixed an explosive charge to the M.L.'s planking. Then the destroyer, drew away, turned and headed out to sea, taking the deepwater Ostend channel because of the low water, which led them out through the gap in the net defense.

At exactly four o'clock *Warwick* hit a mine. It broke her back seventy feet from the stern, gave her a 30 degree list to port and an appearance of imminent disaster. On board, Crutchley picked up his blood-soaked life jacket and put it on again, while from the forecastle the voice of one of the wounded was heard in classic comment: "Oh begor', in the ditch again! That's what comes of shipping a parson—the Admiral ought to have known better!"

The immediate situation was brought under control by swift thought on the part of Engineer Lieutenant Rampling who readjusted trim by flooding the starboard fuel tanks, and vigorous emergency action by the *Warwick*'s crew. When stability had been restored and it became apparent that the ship was not about to plunge to the bottom, *Velox* was lashed alongside, *Whirlwind* took her in tow and *Trident* cruised to the eastward to keep watch for the nine enemy destroyers, which if on dawn patrol would be in a position to make an effective killing.

Flotilla orders in the event of an attack were short to the point of curtness and impossible to misunderstand: *Warwick* was to be slipped from tow and the other three destroyers turn into the attack immediately. As this would almost certainly result in the loss of *Warwick,* the wounded were all transferred to *Velox* but Keyes remained where he was, and so did Crutchley—"who thought he might be useful in case of trouble."

The enemy destroyers did not put in an appearance and thus missed the last chance of an even local victory offered to the German Navy. Just before five o'clock

Keyes sent out a wireless message—in clear, for all *Warwick*'s code and cypher books had gone in the furnace before entering enemy waters—ordering various captains to steam towards a point only identifiable upon their own charts for the night's operation. By seven o'clock *Warwick* had met them and was safe under the protection of heavy guns.

Operation V.S. was over.

## Epilogue

A THIRD attempt against Ostend was agreed to by the Admiralty, planned and put in hand by Keyes and his staff, and the two ships to be used, *Sappho* again, and *Swiftsure,* were actually tried out with various items of special equipment which had been developed from the experience gained on the previous attempts. Then, towards the end of the month, Admiral Wemyss informed Keyes that in view of the latest appreciation of the position by Naval Intelligence, it would appear that the additional advantages now to be gained were insufficient to justify the risk to life and limb.

To this Keyes agreed—for although he hated to give up, he hated far more the idea of lives lost unnecessarily. Data supplied by aerial photographs, examination of prisoners, and agents' reports from occupied territories indicated the percentage of operational success still to be achieved seemed so small as to render further effort rather pointless. It had never been expected that all craft, regardless of size, could be sealed in permanently behind the Belgian coastline, and the Germans had by now removed two piers in the western bank of the Zeebrugge Canal, just abreast and southward of the sunken blockships, and cleared as deep a channel as was possible through the silt under their sterns. Through this channel, small submarines could be warped at high tide, and as the canal system to Ostend could only accommodate small craft anyway, the greatest advantage which could possibly result from another attack at its mouth, would be to increase the traffic at Zeebrugge.

Even Keyes hesitated to mount another attack on the Mole, and in any case there was no need: the really effective ocean-going submarines, and the destroyers, were securely bottled up in Bruges harbor or the adjacent waterways, and likely to remain there.

The basic tactical aims of the operation, therefore, appeared to have been achieved.

This achievement, however, was only a small part of the success which crowned the operations. Napoleon stated that in war the morale is to the physical as three is to one—a contention supported by Clausewitz—and in the case of the Zeebrugge and Ostend raids, the immediate effects upon both military and public morale were widespread and gratifying.

By his operations against the Belgian coast, Keyes restored faith in the Royal Navy, in the Services in general and—most important of all—in the Allies' ability to win the war.

"But above all," says the official historian—who is not generally liberal in his appreciations of actions other than set-piece Naval Fleet battles—"[these operations] brought about that prevision of victory which often in great conflicts appears to be the deciding force—a prevision which is not confined to the combatants, but comes suddenly to the whole attendant world as a revelation of the inevitable end."

While England and her Allies were rejoicing at the resurgence of courage and offensive spirit which these attacks epitomized, Keyes was having immense difficulties in securing either recognition or reward for the individual gallantry of the men who had carried them out.

Always there is a large number of Englishmen of all classes, looking for a small, private, irregular war; during the Second World War, under the direction of a kindred spirit, they were offered ample opportunities for their talents in the Commandos, the private armies, the special forces.

In the World War I there were very few openings for them. The R.F.C. took as many as their establishments could contain, there were the Q ships and the submarines. For a very large number, however, the raid on Zeebrugge offered the first and only chance. When the three columns of the fleet left the Goodwins, there were concentrated in that one striking force a higher proportion of natural, born fighters than any division on the

185

Western Front still contained, or were left behind in the Grand Fleet.

Keyes was a hard man to satisfy in matters of personal courage, and harder to please, but when he had selected the reports of deeds which merited reward even by his high standards, and forwarded the lists to Whitehall, Their Lordships were faced with a request to grant eight V.C.s, 21 D.S.O.s, 29 D.S.C.s, 16 medals for Conspicuous Gallantry, 143 for Distinguished Service, and there were 283 names mentioned in dispatches. The list recommending immediate promotion for service in action contained 56 names—and all this was just for Operation Z.O.: after the night of May 10th the recommendations for V.C.s alone was to be increased by over thirty-five per cent.

The Admiralty was placed in a difficult position. For an action which had lasted only a matter of hours, involved a smaller number of men than were contained in two infantry battalions, and amongst whom there were fewer casualties in killed *and* wounded than many a single battalion had lost in men killed every month since the war broke out, Keyes was requesting more awards than some army divisions had received in four years.

Keyes's ardent spirit was not prepared to yield an inch, and he dealt with it in a very typical manner. He had been created a Knight Commander of the Order of the Bath, as has been related, upon the morning of April 23rd, and it was a particular wish of His Majesty that Keyes should receive the accolade with the due pomp and solemnity of a formal investiture at Buckingham Palace.

Upon every occasion when such an investiture was held and Keyes's presence was requested, he always found some pretext for not attending, until eventually Royal suspicions arose, which when satisfied produced immediate results. Keyes spent a most gratifying few hours at the Admiralty, an edition of the *London Gazette* was ripped from the presses and redrafted, the full list of decorations went through and Keyes accepted his knighthood.

Of the eleven Victoria Crosses awarded, two were posthumous—those of Lieutenant G. N. Bradford of *Iris,* and Lieutenant-Commander A. L. Harrison who had led the last Bluejacket rush along the Mole parapet. Four were granted under Clause Thirteen of the Victoria Cross Warrant which provides for the recipient to be elected by his companions present at the action, when it is considered that the corporate bravery of a naval or military unit has earned the Cross. Carpenter was chosen by the naval officers, Captain Bamford by the Royal Marines, and Leading Seaman McKenzie and Serjeant Finch received the men's nominations.

The other recipients were Dick Sandford of *C 3,* and Lieutenant Dean of *M.L. 282* for Operation Z.O., and Lieutenants Crutchley, Bourke and Drummond for the second attempt at Ostend. The citations for these awards are contained in the appendix to this volume.

Billyard-Leake and Bonham Carter both received the D.S.O., and so did John Howell-Price, Cooke of the Royal Marines, Peshall the Padre, Dallas Brooks, and Helyar, in addition to those already mentioned in the text. The only immediate promotion was Carpenter's, whose acting rank of captain was confirmed within hours of the return to Dover, but Rosoman went up to Commander as soon as he came out of hospital, Francis Sandford did so after the second Ostend raid, and eventually Sneyd of the *Thetis* put up his fourth stripe.

But the war was soon to end, immediate demobilization scattered the "hostilities only" people far and wide, and not too long afterwards the "Geddes Axe" and other schemes of short sight and poor repute were to chop fine timber away from the Naval Oak. Billyard-Leake spent a few years in Submarines and left the Navy in 1929. He returned to the Service during the Second World War, spent some time in Lisbon as assistant naval attaché, then went to Chungking as naval attaché. He died in Kenya in May, 1956, and joined what has inevitably and naturally become the larger proportion of his St. George's Day shipmates.

The Sandford brothers went far too soon, for Dick was to die of typhoid in Grangetown Hospital only six months after he had blown up the viaduct, and Francis, by then a captain, followed him in February, 1926. With sad coincidence, two of the Zeebrugge V.C.s died within three weeks of each other: Leading Seaman McKenzie, having recovered from his wounds, caught the dreadful Spanish influenza and died three days later on November 3, 1918, twenty days before Dick Sandford.

But not all of the gallant band have left us yet, and some of them have gone from strength to strength. Bonham Carter asked for command of a destroyer after Zeebrugge and much to his amazement and delight was given the *Shark,* which happened to be the Navy's latest. Later, in *Petersfield,* he had as his first lieutenant the indomitable Crutchley and was only to regret it on the occasions when visitors on board, faced by two officers, one fair, fresh-faced with a charming and boyish smile, the other bearded, stern, and wearing the purple ribbon, made a not unnatural mistake and assumed that Crutchley was the commanding officer.

The solution seemed to be for Bonham Carter to go either gray or bald, but the life he was to lead was hardly conducive to this for, after a spell in the Mediterranean, he was posted to the South African station where for some years he had a magnificent time, steadily progressing up the ladder of Naval promotion all the while. Shortly after the outbreak of the Second World War he was appointed Naval Secretary to Mr. Churchill, but the time was to come only too soon when naval expansion, and some early tragic losses, were to place a high premium upon organizational and executive experience.

Soon Bonham Carter's flag was flying at Halifax, and convoys making the desperate North Atlantic crossing from west to east did so under his direction. He was to retire after the war as full admiral and his career of cheerful service was rightly rewarded with a K.C.B., which gives to the Cricket Club of which he is president and the various committees upon which he sits with shrewd good humor that little extra dignity so dear to the heart of rural England.

The Navy list reveals that Admiral Sir Victor Crutchley is still a power to be reckoned with in whatever part of the world he has settled: if they didn't before, the natives by now will regard the Royal Navy with the awe and respect which is its proper due. One could almost wish he'd decided to live in Cairo.

Captain Carpenter wrote a book upon his own part in the blocking of Zeebrugge, and toured America during the 1920's lecturing upon the raid. He retired from the Navy with the rank of Rear-Admiral in 1929, was for some years president of the Zeebrugge Association, and it was not until the end of 1955 that he at last went to join the sixty officers and men of *Vindictive*'s crew who did not live to see the extent of their own victory.

And what of *Vindictive* herself?

The Germans dismantled much of her superstructure before they evacuated Ostend, stripping out all the machinery and scrap metal they could use, cutting away parts of her plating. But the main bulk was still there when the Armistice was signed, and as she was not in the fairway there was no pressing need for her to be moved. Ostend still remembers the night of May 10th, and *Vindictive*'s name on a part of her hull forms a monument which keeps the memory fresh.

*Iphigenia* and *Intrepid* were eventually removed from the mouth of the Zeebrugge canal in the middle 1920's, but it was not until January, 1921, that the channel was sufficiently cleared to allow normal commercial use, and there was still much work to be done before the last remains of the blockships were dragged from the canal bed.

There is certainly no wish on the part of the Zeebrugge inhabitants to forget all about Operation Z.O. On St. George's Day, 1925, a fine memorial was unveiled by the King of the Belgians at the shore end of the Mole which had been subscribed for by British, French, and Belgians. The Germans demolished it when they reoccupied the Flanders coast, but native ingenuity and enterprise has replaced it with an even more constant reminder of the attack: if you wish to spend the night in Zeebrugge you will be well advised to patronize the "Hotel Vindictive."

There remains the man who brought it all about.

During the rest of the summer of 1918 he stepped up

even further the activities of the Dover Patrol and by June the U-boat menace had at last been defeated. It was not until Keyes had taken command at Dover that there was any sign of slackening in the dreadful stranglehold of this arm of the German Navy: six months later it was broken, and within a year, after coming nearer to defeat than at any other time, the Allies imposed the Armistice terms upon a beaten Germany.

It is fascinating to study the ingenuity, the special pleading and the mental contortions of those who have sought for so long to prove that Keyes had nothing whatsoever to do with the successful prosecution of the Great War. It was not a case of jealousy, of that one be-comes convinced after a fairly short examination of the arguments, and of the personalities concerned—but after some time a common psychological thread is perceived to link the events, the characters, the mental attitudes.

Disillusion and disappointment lay such a heavy blight so early upon the dreams of youth, that by middle age we fear even to hope and still less to believe that sim-plicity, honesty, and courage are enough. Life has taught us that to be successful we need influence. We need the cunning of an animal, the devious insight of a Machiavelli and the luck of the Devil: with all these Fate's blind malice may be temporarily outwitted, the masterminds among us managing to buy complete security at the mere cost of their souls. But we learnt in tears and terror as we grew up, that right was not might, that St. George would be better advised to enter a defensive alliance with the dragon than to try to defeat him, and that eager youth is no match for authoritative old age.

But Keyes *was* eager youth—all his life.

He was as uninterested in the principles behind politics or even ethics as the hero of a boy's magazine serial, and he would lose his right leg for a friend—in fact once in his career he was for several minutes in imminent danger of exactly that misfortune, because he refused to move six feet away from one of his officers who was trapped by a broken cable. To him, people were the factors of impor-tance and reality, not the systems by which they may or may not achieve happiness and success. He would have

190

died for his King or his Country without a moment's hesitation, but it is doubtful whether he ever really grasped the implications of that useful word "expediency."

Thus for Keyes—with *his* attitude and qualities—to have been right, and to have played a major and successful part in defeating the enemy, entails an admission that our boyhood dreams were truth after all and that our ideals should have been kept untarnished, instead of being allowed to dull into the middle-aged creed that God is on the side of the big battalions.

And this would never do.

By the end of the war, Keyes's place in the Naval hierarchy appeared certain and unchallengeable: Rosslyn Wemyss was still First Sea Lord and his successor would obviously be David Beatty. That Keyes should follow in the supreme Naval appointment seemed inevitable. In the meantime there were the few last years of executive command at sea still to be enjoyed to the full.

For two years Keyes commanded a battle-cruiser force at Rosyth. There followed six months rest on half pay, then four years as Deputy Chief of Naval Staff and a Lord Commissioner of the Admiralty. In May 1925, he took command of the Mediterranean Fleet.

It was during these years at Malta that he unconsciously laid the foundations for the attacks which were later leveled against him. A keen and expert polo player, he encouraged the sport among his junior officers. His enemies interpreted this as a sign of snobbery and whispered that a poor polo player could never hope for promotion under Keyes's command. When the Socialist government was returned to power, Keyes's reputation as an eager fighter and a man with aristocratic leanings counted heavily against him. Though in line for promotion, he was passed over, and the government chose Sir Frederick Field as First Sea Lord. For Keyes, who still had some years to go before his retirement, this event marked the end of his career in the Navy.

Keyes retired in 1931 and occupied himself with writing his *Memoirs*. At the outbreak of World War II he was recalled to duty and served briefly as Director of

Combined Operations, where he organized and trained the Commando forces. Once again, however, his boyish determination to get at the enemy brought him into conflict with the strategists. After months of toil and frustration, Mr. Churchill, giving way at last to the wishes of his advisors, relieved Keyes of his post.

The rest of the war was spent in helpful but unimportant war work, and in 1943, at Mr. Churchill's representation, Keyes became a baron. He chose as his title "Baron Keyes of Zeebrugge and Dover in the County of Kent" and as supporters for his coat of arms, a sailor of the Royal Navy in working rig and a Royal Marine equipped for raiding.

It was almost the end of the road. He saw the defeat of Hitler's Germany, but was mercifully spared the picture of the dismemberment of the British Empire and the collapse of his country's influence which followed so quickly afterwards—for he died in his sleep early in the morning of December 28, 1945.

Keyes will always be the subject of controversy and argument because he stood for direct, simple action. He was of the opinion that wars are best won quickly, never by running away or waiting, always by sustained but varying attack.

To hold these views and to act upon them demands spirit and courage, and these are attributes which wither in most men as their powers of rationalization and self-deception grow, while at the same time they attain influence and the position from which to make their protestations heard. Keyes has frequently been compared with Nelson, and possibly if he had died at Zeebrugge he would by now have been as deeply venerated: but living, he could correct the interpretations by which others would strive to justify their own principles of action in terms of his success. Therefore his success must not be acknowledged.

But in one of the letters received by his widow are these words:

"His voice was the voice of England because it always rang true, like precious metal tempered in the fire."